PLAYING WITH A

FOOTBALL

By MORRIS A. SHIRTS
& THOMAS R. KINGSFORD
of Southern Utah State College

 STERLING PUBLISHING CO., INC. NEW YORK

OTHER BOOKS OF INTEREST

Guinness Sports Record Book
Warm Up for Little League Baseball

Athletic Institute Series

Baseball	Gymnastics
Basketball	Table Tennis
Girls' Basketball	Tumbling and Trampolining
Girls' Gymnastics	Wrestling

CONTENTS

BEFORE YOU BEGIN

"Playing with a Football" is written to help you understand the basic elements of the game and develop the skills necessary to enjoy playing football in a back yard, vacant lot, park, or playground. You ought to learn the game while young.

You are bound to get a thrill by being a part of a team effort, especially when you see how your own effort makes the team a success. In the process, you will learn how to watch college and professional football games with understanding. Football can be a great and exciting sport to watch, as it requires not only strength, but skill and cleverness, both in planning and working out plays on offense and defense.

The purpose of this book is to help you develop a healthy attitude toward football by teaching you the fundamentals first in a game that is like football, but with fewer than eleven players per side, although it follows all the basic rules of football.

Dana X. Bible, a great football teacher, once pointed out that there was no greater game than football to teach you how to control and command your own powers.

- It will help you make your body strong.
- It will teach you the need to follow orders.
- It will give you practice in making decisions.
- It will show you the value of placing the interest of others above your own.
- It will teach you how to take disappointment and still strive to win.

- It will impress you with the value of courage.

A few years ago the Rules Committee of the National Collegiate Athletic Association (NCAA) developed what is called "The Football Code." Part of it is re-written here to help explain to you the way football should be played.

SPORTSMANSHIP. It is your duty to obey the rules. If you disobey a rule on purpose you are playing unfairly and are not a good sport, whether you are caught or not.

FOLLOWING THE RULES. No matter what the coach or other players say or do, don't break rules. If you or others are dishonest or cheat, it is not fair to the boys, the game, or the other players. Officials try to see that everybody plays by the rules, and you should respect them. Officials sometimes make mistakes which could affect the outcome of the game, but they do the best job they can. You must learn to accept their judgment. If there is a question about the call of an official, let your team captain discuss it with the officials. That is his business. Let him do it alone.

HOLDING AND HITTING. Certain rules cover the use of hands, arms, legs, and feet—observe them. You are not allowed to hold or hit another player to keep him from doing his job. If holding were permitted, football would not be football—it would be more like wrestling. If players were permitted to punch each other with their hands or fists, it would be more like boxing rather than football. The aim of the game is move the ball down the field by clever thinking and playing, rather than by holding and punching.

A FAIR START. It is unfair for one team to start moving the ball before the other team is ready. Each has to have a "fair chance." Secret signals that cheat on the other team should not be used.

UNFAIR SHIFTING. Making the other team move before the ball is snapped is unfair, if done with the idea of tricking them into breaking the rules. Clever signals aimed at keeping the other team from guessing what you are going to do is all right, but not to deceive them.

FAKING INJURIES. If you are injured you may need, and should have, immediate attention. It is unfair for anyone to make an official think he is injured when he isn't. It is unfair to the other team, and it is unfair to a player who really might be injured.

LOUD-MOUTHING. There is no rule against it, but you should not talk to members of the other team in a disrespectful way. Football is intended to make gentlemen out of boys. Encouragement and respect for good work does this better than razzing. Winning by being skillful at the game should be the aim, and not trying to win by loud talk.

Football is a great sport, but when players (and coaches) break the code upon which it must be played, it ceases to be a sport. Playing the game can teach the thrill of winning, but also how to take defeat. Play fair!

1. THROWING THE BALL

Although football is a team sport with a captain and a group of players all working together, the skill of the individual player determines the outcome of the game. A missed block, a poor tackle, a bad pass, or a bad punt can mean the difference between defeat and victory for the team. What are some of these individual skills so necessary for good football?

Do you know why an American football has such an unusual shape, why it isn't round like a basketball or a soccer ball? The main reason is so that it can be thrown. You can't throw a basketball very far because it is too big and round. Once the football was round . . . almost like a basketball. But soon after the Notre Dame team "invented" the forward pass in 1913 in a game against Army, the coaches and players felt that the ball was not shaped very well for throwing far. As more teams began to use the forward pass, the shape and size of the football was gradually changed.

It still takes a lot of practice to throw it well. A good pass is not only accurate, but easy to catch. Here are some pointers to help you.

The Grip

The first thing to learn in throwing a football well is how to hold or grip it. A good passer has big, strong hands, which helps him hold the ball. If your hands are small, like most boys, you might want to use a ball which is smaller than those used by high school, college and pro football players. If you can't handle one of the regular-sized balls easily, be sure to borrow or buy one of the smaller-sized balls while learning to throw. If you are buying a new football, don't get a full-sized one. However, don't use the little "toy" balls 5 to 6 inches long which can be bought in the drug store. Get one of the small-sized footballs made for boys, which is available in sporting goods stores. In the "Ford Punt, Pass and Kick Contest," for example, these smaller balls are used for the younger boys.

To grip the ball right, place the little finger of your throwing hand on the laces of the ball, just a little back of the center of the laces—on about the 5th lacing from the front end of the ball. Place your next finger on the nearest lace (the 4th from the front). Your next two fingers are not placed on the laces at all. Place your index finger, that is your pointing finger, near the end or point of the football. Your thumb should be spread away from your fingers and placed on the ball under your index finger, near the back end of the ball. The palm of your hand should not be touching the ball at all. The ball, you see, is held between the ends of the fingers and the thumb.

PASSING GRIP: Place your little finger on the fourth lace from the front of the ball. Place your index finger near the end of the ball.

THE PALM of your hand should not be touching the ball when you throw it.

YOUR PASSING ARM should continue moving downward after you release the ball. This is called follow-through.

After you have tried holding the football this way, you will immediately find that you have to have strong hands to be a good passer. If you really want to, you can develop more strength in your hands. Try doing push-ups on your fingertips or practice squeezing a soft rubber ball with your hands. Keep the ball in your pocket and squeeze it as you walk along.

Another way you can make your throwing hand stronger is to hold the ball in the throwing grip, palm down, and let the ball drop from your fingers. Then try to catch it with the same hand in the football grip before the ball hits the ground.

Passing

Next, take your stance with the ball held in the throwing grip as explained above. Bring your arm straight back alongside your ear. As you do this, bring your throwing or pivot foot (right foot if you are right-handed) back and place the weight of your body on it. Your shoulders should be pointed in the same direction as you are going to throw. Hold out the other arm in the same direction to help give you balance. Point your forward foot in this direction also.

Your feet should be spread apart about as wide as your shoulders, no wider. As you throw, shift the weight of your body to your front foot. You can't throw well with the weight of your body on your back foot.

As you begin the throw, you lead with the elbow of your throwing arm. Point it in the direction of the throw. Your hand with the ball should come forward within 3 to 6 inches of your ear. Your wrist should be held stiff until the ball leaves your hand.

The release point occurs as your wrist is quickly "snapped" or turned (almost like a baseball pitcher throwing a curve) forward and downward. Your index finger should point in the exact direction of the pass as the ball leaves your hand. This gives the ball a little "spin" or "spiral" to help it fly through the air. Your throwing arm should keep on moving downward in a nice, smooth motion.

As you release the ball, you should keep the following things in mind:

1. The ball should be pointed upward just a little. This lets the air get under it like it does with an airplane wing, and this helps it fly through the air.

2. Try to give the ball a little spin. It needs a little, not too much. A ball that is spinning fast is harder to catch than one spinning slowly. Practice will show you how to put just enough on it to keep it from tumbling through the air.

3. Try to "lead your receiver" a little. This means that you should try to throw the ball ahead of the receiver, to the spot where he will be when the ball gets there. The football and the receiver have to arrive at the same place at the same time.

4. Try to aim the ball so the receiver can catch it at the height of his head, shoulder, or chest. If he has to jump for it, or dive for it, or pick it up at his knees, he might not be able to hang on to it.

5. Learn how to "fake" your pass. Pump your arm with the ball to make it look as if you are going to throw to one man, then at the last minute change and throw to another.

Back-yard Practice

To be good at throwing the football, you must practice, but you must only practice the right things. If you practice doing something wrong, then you will learn to do it the wrong way. Follow the instructions here and you will learn the right way to do it—then practice. Here are some ideas to help you have more fun with your practicing.

TARGET: Hang an old tire from a tree or basketball backboard.

Hang an old automobile tire with a rope to a tree limb or a basketball backboard. Hang it so it is about 6 feet from the ground. Put a net 6 feet behind it if you can. Then, practice throwing the ball through the center of the tire. When you are able to hit the hole 9 out of 10 times, back up a few feet and practice some more. As you improve, let the tire swing back and forth, and try to hit the hole as the tire is swinging. You can hold contests with your dad, brothers, or friends. See who can put the ball through the center of the tire the most times out of ten tries. If you can hit the hole in the swinging tire 8 out of 10 tries at a distance of 25 yards, you are good enough to make almost any boys' team.

More fun is to play "fox and geese" with a football. It's not a contest, but still it is exciting. You need at least one other boy to do this. Three or four would make it more interesting. All the boys start by running in the same direction in a large circle. Make the circle as large as your playing area will allow, but not too large to throw across. The boy who has the ball throws it across the circle to another boy without stopping. The boy who catches it throws it back across the circle. No one is allowed to stop running or run or turn backwards (unless just two are playing). You must catch and throw the ball on the run.

After running in one direction for a while, all can change and run in the other direction.

Throwing a football requires a strong arm. Squeezing a rubber ball and doing push-ups, as explained earlier, will help. Here is another action exercise to help develop muscles in your throwing arm. Put one knee (right knee for right-handers and left knee for left-handers) on the ground and place the other foot a little bit forward. Now throw the ball in the direction your forward foot is pointed. This makes you throw with the muscles of your arm, back and wrist and develops throwing strength. You might try throwing to another boy and take turns with him.

2. CATCHING AND RUNNING WITH THE BALL

The football has to be passed and caught on every football play. It is impossible to run a football play, even a running play, without passing the ball. Did you know that? The Quarterback must be able to "catch" the ball from the Center on every play. The "snap" from the Center is actually a very short pass, and the Quarterback, or the Running Back, must be able to catch it. If the Quarterback hands the ball to a Running Back, the Running Back must be able to "catch" it. If the Quarterback throws a long pass, the receiver must be able to catch it. Let's start at the beginning—when the Quarterback "catches" the ball from the Center.

Getting the Ball from the Center

Most of the time, the Quarterback gets the ball from the Center while stooping over him. Sometimes he stands back and gets a "long pass" from the Center, but most of the time you see the Quarterback working close to the Center. He stands with his feet spread apart, with his throwing foot back a little (right one if he is right-handed and the left one if he is left-

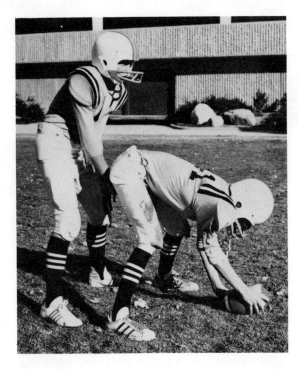

QUARTERBACK STANCE: Place your hands right under the seat of the Center. Stand up close.

handed). The toe of his throwing foot should be about even with the middle of his other foot. This is to give him better balance. His knees are bent just a little, and his body is bent forward. His hands are under the Center and his head is raised so he can watch the defensive men and his own teammates.

The most important thing he does can't be seen. This is what he does with his hands. They must be held just right and the same way each time or he can't get the ball from the Center without fumbling it. He has to get the ball without even looking at it. That seems pretty hard—to catch a pass without looking at the ball, but he can do it easily, if he does it right.

A QUARTERBACK'S HANDS when he gets the ball from the Center should be held this way with thumbs together, fingers spread and palms down.

THE CENTER is ready to snap the ball. His left hand will turn it to the left and help guide it into the hands of the Quarterback.

Let's see how you as Quarterback would do it.

First of all, you must hold your two hands together in the right way. Place your throwing hand out in front of you with your fingers stretched out and your palm down. Now turn your other hand so your palm is up and put your thumbs together. The first knuckle of your top thumb should fit between the first and second knuckle of your other thumb. The fingers of your bottom hand should be pointing toward the ground. Keep both wrists "locked" and push your hands and wrists under the Center. Your top hand should push or lift up against the Center and be held tightly there—right under his crotch. This tells the

GETTING THE PASS from the Center: The fingers of the Quarterback's bottom hand snap shut on the ball, pushing it against his top hand.

Center where your hand is so he has a target. Don't be bashful—this is the way it has to be done.

You have to practice so you can put your top hand under his seat exactly the same way every time. Your top hand must not move. It stays still. Your bottom hand is the one that moves. It works like a door and closes tightly on the ball as the Center snaps it against your top hand. You should practice with the Center so he can snap the ball to you the same way each time. The ball should snap into your top hand with the laces up and against your fingers so you won't have to turn the ball around to get it in the passing position.

Your next move is also important. You should move forward with the Center as he charges into the line. You don't follow him, unless you are trying to do a Quarterback "sneak." Just move your hands and body

THE BALL SNAP: The Center passes the ball, laces up, so the Quarterback's top hand encloses the laces.

slightly forward as he charges. You do this to make sure you have the ball tightly in your hands.

Most of the fumbles that take place when the ball is snapped from the Center, happen because the Quarterback starts to move back away from the Center before he has the ball. As you move back, you should pull the ball right back into your stomach, getting the fingers of your passing hand over the laces. Keep your elbows close to your body and your body forward a little. This will help you hold onto the ball in case a defensive lineman comes crashing through the line and tackles you. It also helps you hide the

AS HE ACCEPTS the ball from the Center, the Quarterback's hands should be on the ball this way.

ball. You can run with it, give it to someone else, or pass it.

You can see how important it is for the Quarterback to be able to "catch" this "pass" from the Center each time. You should practice this over and over until you can do it right each time without even looking at the ball or the Center. You must be able to do it without looking.

The Hand-off

After the Quarterback gets the ball from the Center, he can do three things with it. He can run with it, pass it, or give it to someone else. When he gives it to someone else, it is actually a very short pass, a special kind of pass. He places it in the arms of the other player, who is running by him. This is called the "hand-off" and, if it is to work properly, the Running Back, who gets the ball must "catch" it in a very special way. This is how you should do it if you are the Running Back.

First of all, you and the Quarterback must know on which side you are going to run, because if you run by the Quarterback on his right side, and he turns left, you can't get the ball. You ought to practice it both ways, on his right and on his left.

As you run toward the Quarterback, aim yourself so you can pass by him very closely. Don't touch him, just barely miss him, and make yourself a basket! Have you ever seen a football player with a basket? Of course, you couldn't take a basket on the field with you, but you have to make one—out of your arms, hands, and fingers.

When passing on the Quarterback's left, you stretch out your left hand, palm up, with your little finger towards your belt buckle, with your thumb sticking out in front and your fingers curled up just a little. Your left elbow should be away from your body and forward a little.

Now place your right hand in front of your body,

palm down, with your thumb pointing to or touching your chest and your fingers stretched out but curled a little. This hand, your right one, will now be just about over your left wrist, and will help your left arm form the bottom of the basket, to catch the ball and keep it from squirting out.

Now raise your right elbow up high. The open end of the basket will be right under your right elbow. Now stoop over, or lean forward as you run by the Quarterback. If you have made this basket properly, with the top open wide, he can push or shove the ball into it as you pass by him. As you feel the ball fit firmly in your basket, shut the lid on it by dropping your right elbow and clamp your right hand and left arm tightly over the ball. Your left hand should also grasp the ball. In this position, you can charge straight into the line. Don't stand up straight. Keep low with both feet digging fast and hard. Practice hand-offs when passing on both sides of the Quarterback. You would of course use your other hands passing on the Quarterback's right side.

The Quarterback may want the ball back after he gives it to you, so there are times when you don't want to close the lid on your basket. This is called a "fake." The Quarterback may want the defensive men to think he has given you the ball, so they will chase you while he runs with the ball in another direction.

You and the Quarterback must decide whether to fake the hand-off. If you should decide to fake the hand-off and then you forget and close the lid on the

THE "BASKET" which the Running Back makes for a proper hand-off from the Quarterback is exactly like this.

THE HAND-OFF: The Quarterback places the ball in the Running Back's basket exactly like this.

basket, he would have a hard time getting it back, wouldn't he? To make a good fake, he must actually put the ball in the top of your basket, then pull it out. After he pulls it out, you must close the lid on the basket and charge forward just as if you had the ball in the basket.

As the Quarterback gets the ball from the Center, he pulls it into his stomach and turns to his left (or right) so the defensive men cannot see the ball. Then as you pass by him, he moves his rear foot back out of the way so he won't trip you, and shoves the ball into your basket as you go by. You need to do this together—this is called "timing." He can't get the ball into your basket if you go by him before he is ready, or if he gets ready long before you go by him. Practice it until you can do it together, just at the right time. Practice fakes. Let him put the ball in your basket, then he should pull it out to pass or to run with it. You might practice having two Running Backs go by the Quarterback, with both making a basket. He could place the ball in your basket, then pull it out and put it in the basket of the other Running Back.

The Quarterback must keep his eyes on your basket during the hand-off. He can then shove the ball in with both hands, or with one hand, but his aim must be perfect. The lower hand usually shoves the ball and the top hand guides it into the basket. Your basket is moving fast and he must be able to put the ball in it without missing.

CATCHING A LONG PASS: The receiver's arms and fingers are stretched out to scoop the ball into his arms and body.

You should learn to take the hand-off from both sides, so practice it both ways. If you are right-handed, you will prefer to take the ball on your left side by running to the right of the quarterback. If you or the Quarterback is left-handed, it would be more natural for him to give the ball to you under your right elbow as you pass by him on his left. But, you must practice the hand-off on both sides, or the opposing team will always know which side to defend against. Get somebody to practice the hand-off with you. Take turns. One of you be the Quarterback and the other the Running Back. Then trade places. Practice this whenever you have a chance. Lots of fumbles take place on the hand-off because it is not made properly.

Catching the Long Pass

Like other passes or ball exchanges between two players, catching a long pass requires special skills. A good Quarterback is good because someone catches his passes. If the passes he throws aren't caught, he has a poor passing record. No pass is good if it isn't caught. Let's see if, as the pass receiver, you can learn how to catch a long pass correctly.

First of all, remember that although you must reach with your arms, you should use your hands and fingers in catching a pass. Your arms are great for holding the ball only after your hands catch it, but they are not much good for catching. Keep your arms and fingers relaxed (and not stiff) so they can move quickly and easily. Keep your fingers stretched out and curled a little, with the palms of your hands toward you. Make a basket out of both hands and fingers. As the ball touches your fingers and hands, fold them against the ball, and pull it into your arms, pushing it against your body, so it won't be jarred loose when someone tackles or bumps you.

Remember to keep your eyes on the ball until it is in your hands. This is hard to do, especially when you are running, as each step jars your eyes a little. It is hard to run and still keep your eyes on the ball, but good pass receivers can do it. If you try to look at anything else, or if you think about anything else when trying to catch a pass, you will probably miss it. If you try to watch the man who is going to tackle you, or if you think about him, you will miss the ball.

When you run down the field for a long pass, you usually know where the Quarterback is going to try to throw it, and you need to be there when the ball gets there. You should be able to look back over your shoulder and see the ball coming to you. Let it come over your shoulder and fall into your outstretched hands. As soon as you have it in your hands, pull it into your body and keep right on running toward the goal line. Sometimes you might have to jump high in the air to get it. Sometimes you might have to change your direction a little, slow down a little, or speed up a little to get in the right place. Since you only have a

CATCHING A LONG, LOW PASS: The receiver must scoop the ball into his hands and arms and against his body.

few seconds to get to the right place, you should start from a 3-point stance (see page 58) and, like a sprinter charging out of his starting blocks, race down the field as fast as you can.

If there is a defensive player chasing you and trying to get the ball, try to fake him away from the spot where the Quarterback intends to throw the ball. You can do this by running in the wrong direction, then suddenly turning to run toward the right place. As a Pass Catcher you might run slowly at first, to make the defensive players think you are not going to catch the ball, then suddenly speed up and race to the right spot.

It takes a lot of practice to learn how to catch long passes. You must work closely with the Quarterback so you both know where he is going to throw the ball. You must learn how to fake the defensive players out of the way, and still get there in time to catch it. You have to learn how to make last-minute changes to get under the ball just at the right time. So find someone to practice with, and practice until you can do it.

The Full Pass from the Center

If you are a kicker, or a Quarterback, sometimes you need to catch the ball back from the scrimmage line quite a way as the Center snaps it. You usually don't try to catch it over your shoulder like you do in a long pass. You stand facing the Center with both hands out in front of you. If the ball comes to you above your waist, the palms of your hands should be facing forward with thumbs together. If the ball comes to you below your waist, the palms of your hands should be facing up with your little fingers together. The same thing is true, if you are catching a short pass from the Quarterback. Unless you are going to kick it, catch the ball in your hands and pull it down and into your body so it won't squirt away from you when you are bumped or tackled.

Here are some general rules for catching passes:

■ Use your hands and fingers to catch the ball—not your arms or body.

■ Keep your arms and hands relaxed. You can't catch with "sticks."

■ Use both hands to catch the ball.

■ Keep your fingers spread wide.

■ Know where the pass is to be thrown and get there on time.

■ Fake defenders away from the ball. Use a change of pace or change of direction to make defenders think you are going to do one thing—then do another.

■ Know where the ball is and keep your eye on it while it is coming into your fingers.

■ Run to catch the ball without stretching out your arms until the ball has arrived.

■ Pull the ball into your body and hang onto it tightly with your arms hugging it after you get it.

Running with the Ball

After you take the hand-off or catch the long pass, your job is only half done. You must now run. There are two different ways to run with the ball: either you

CRASHING: The ball carrier holds the ball with both hands so he won't get it knocked loose.

try to crash through the scrimmage line, or you run across or down the field trying to reach the goal line.

Crashing through the Scrimmage Line

You must hold the ball tightly in crashing so it won't squirt out of your hands when you are bumped and tackled. Hold it tightly across your stomach in the basket you have just learned to make. Holding the ball as horizontal as possible, your arms should be across the ball, with one over the top of it and the other under the bottom of it. If you are right-handed, your right arm will usually be the one under the ball with your right hand grasping the end of the ball, as far left as just above your left hip. Your left arm will be over the top of the ball with your left hand grasping the center or other end of the ball just above your right hip. You should lean your body forward from the waist, and you should take short, powerful steps. In this position, it is almost impossible for a tackler to knock the ball out of your hands. You won't be able to run fast and you won't be able to change directions quickly, but you can run hard and powerfully.

You must be able to see where you are going, so when you lean your body forward, don't lower your head too much. Don't let your chin quite touch your chest. If you do, you can't see where you are going, and if you run into someone with your head, you could hurt your neck. So keep your head up a little— just high enough to be able to see above the top bar of your face guard. This way you will see the holes your blockers are making for you so you can charge through them as they clear the way.

If the defensive team is good, you will usually be stopped as you get to the line of scrimmage, or just as you get through it. Good runners will keep digging hard with their feet, trying to get as far as they can. Even when they are tackled, they keep trying. Sometimes if the tackle is not a good one, the runner can break away from it and keep right on running. So when you are tackled, don't stop running. Try to keep going. Try not to let yourself be pushed or carried backward—drive forward until you hit the ground. Once you get through the scrimmage line, look for open spaces and try to get to them. For this, you need to do some "open-field" running.

Open-field Running

In this kind of running, you are usually trying to get around the scrimmage line or down the field to the goal line after you have caught a pass. You must be able to run fast and keep from being tackled. When you are tackled, you must hold onto the ball and not let it get knocked out of your hands.

First of all, learn how to hold the ball correctly. The best way is to hold it in one arm tight against your body. Hold one end of the ball with one hand with your fingers locked around it. Tuck the other end of the ball into your armpit. There should be no daylight showing between your ribs and the ball. If you are running down field on the right sideline, hold the ball on your right side. If you are running down the

RUNNING DOWNFIELD: The ball carrier has one end tucked into his armpit and his hand over the other end.

A   B   C

OPEN-FIELD RUNNING: How the ball carrier switches the ball from one arm to the other. In A, he has it under his right arm, and is just starting out. In B, he is changing it over, holding with both arms. In C, he has finished the switch, and all along he continues to run.

left sideline, hold the ball on your left side. Try to keep your body between the ball and the tacklers, so they have to tackle your body and not the ball. When you are tackled, concentrate on hanging onto the ball tightly. Don't let it go.

You can use your other arm to help keep the tacklers away from you. You must not use your fist, but try to push or shove him away from you with your open hand and a straight or bent arm.

Practice running with the ball held in either hand. When you can do this well, practice changing it from one side to the other while running. Practice it while standing still until you can do it easily, then try it while running. This is hard to do, but if you can learn to do it well, you will be a better open-field runner.

All you do is to change the ball from one side to the other, placing the lower end of the ball in the other armpit. You need to keep the ball protected during this change-over so you won't drop it accidentally or when you're tackled. Try it this way: Reach over with your free hand and grasp the end of the ball which is in your armpit. At the same time, move the ball across your chest, using your bottom hand to guide the lower end of the ball into your other armpit. Your other hand should pull the top end of the ball downward across your chest to the other side. Lock the ball in the new position as tightly as it was in the old position. All this should be done while you are running, without stopping.

Here are some good rules for all runners:

- Always hang onto the ball tightly with both hands, so you won't lose it when tackled.
- Run with your blockers. Let them clear the way for you.
- Look for the open holes and run through them.
- Keep your body between the ball and your tacklers.
- Fake likely tacklers out of the way. Change your direction, change your speed, make them think you are going to do one thing—then do another. Make it hard for them to make a good tackle on you.
- Drive for the extra yard.

Loose Balls

In almost any football game, someone drops a ball. What should you do if you see a loose ball on the ground? Do you pick it up and run with it or fall on it?

If you are near the ball all by yourself, you should pick it up and run with it. Stoop over as you run by the ball and scoop it up with both hands. Tuck it into your armpit and run towards the goal line.

If there are other players around you, the best thing to do is to fall on the ball. Dive on it, scooping it against your body with both hands. Turn your body a little so you can double up and wrap yourself around the ball. Pull your knees and your head and shoulders toward each other with the ball between them and hold it tightly with both arms so no one can get it away from you.

3. PUNTING AND KICKING

To be able to kick and punt well in a football game often spells the difference between winning and losing. Kicking an extra point after touchdown can win the game. Missing the extra point can lose it. Many times being able to make a field goal wins the football game. Being able to get off long kicks at the "kick-off" is also an important factor in the game. Being able to kick the ball into the area in front of the other team's goal line keeps the ball away from your own goal line. The "quick-kick" and the "punt" also help keep the ball away from your own goal line. In modern football, teams have players who can get off good kicks all the time. These players practice all week long on improving their kicking. On some teams these players do nothing but kick. Would you like to learn how to kick well? You have to want to spend enough time to become a good kicker. If you do, here are some things you must learn.

How to Punt

Punting is kicking the ball without placing it on the ground and without help from another player. You hold the ball and kick it yourself. This is how you do it.

Standing

If you are receiving the ball in a snap from the Center, stand with your hands outstretched, fingers spread out like a basket to catch the ball. The first thing you must do is to catch the ball. (See page 34.)

Keep Your Eye on the Ball

Don't look at anything else, you have to watch the ball and be ready for it as the Center snaps it to you. If you are looking at something else or are scared of getting caught by the other team, or if you blink your eyes just as the ball is snapped, you could miss it. If it is a bad snap from the Center you might not have time to reach it.

Catching and Holding the Ball

When you are standing with your arms stretched out and your hands in front of you, your hands act as a target for the Center. Don't move them until after he has snapped the ball. Catch the ball in both hands, and quickly get into kicking position.

There are two ways to catch and hold the ball for punting. One is to hold it between your hands, each hand along one side of the ball with the middle finger of each hand on the seam pointing to the front of the ball. Of course, the ball is pointed in the direction of the kick. Use both hands to place or guide the ball to the top of your kicking foot as you swing your leg to kick the ball. Just as your foot is about to touch the ball, let go of it with both hands.

The other way to hold the ball is to place one open

WAITING FOR THE SNAP:
When kicking, hold your arms and hands out as a target for the Center.

READY TO PUNT: The laces are on top.

THE KICKER keeps the middle finger of each hand along the middle seam of the ball. He will place the ball on the top of his right foot as he kicks it.

hand on the bottom of the ball and the other on top of the ball, with the ball pointed in the direction you intend to kick it. The fingers of your bottom hand should be on the bottom seam of the ball, your top hand along the strings. As you place the ball on your kicking foot, move your bottom hand away and leave your top hand on the ball to guide it the last few inches to your kicking foot.

With either of these two methods you must raise the front end of the ball a little higher than the rear end. This will help you kick it farther. If it is to be a short punt, hold the ball so the front is a little lower than the rear.

Remember to keep the lacings on the top as you kick the ball.

If your kicking foot kicks the ball on the lacings, it won't go straight. As you get the ball from the Center, turn it between your hands so the lacings are on the top before you kick it.

Taking Steps

The total number of steps you take before you kick the ball is important. You can't kick a ball well without taking steps, but if you take more than two steps, you won't have time to get the ball away before the opposing linemen block it. You must be a "two-step" kicker to be good. It is really $1\frac{1}{2}$ steps, as the first one is a short one. Measure off and stand behind the kicking spot $1\frac{1}{2}$ steps. When you get the ball from the Center, take a short step with your "kicking foot" (the foot you intend to

WHEN KICKING, the top of your foot should hit the ball and not the end of your toe.

use to kick the ball). Then take the large step with your other foot and bring your kicking foot into kicking position. With left-handed boys, the kicking foot is usually the left foot. With right-handed boys, the kicking foot is usually the right foot.

The Kick

It is more important how your leg and foot snap as your foot hits the ball than how hard you kick the ball. Most important is how well the ball and your foot come together. As the kicking motion starts, your kicking leg should be slightly bent. It should swing exactly toward the direction you want to punt. At the moment your foot hits the ball your leg should be "locked" or stiff at the knee and your ankle and the toe of your shoe should be pointed and stretched toward the target. Your leg should swing in a straight line curve toward the direction you want to kick the ball. Your toes should be stretched out pointing toward the direction of the kick.

If you are left-footed, the left lacings of your kicking shoe should hit the bottom of the football. (If right-footed, hit the right lacing holes.) If you want to see how well you do this, make a white chalk line on the middle or bottom seam of the football. As you kick the ball, some of this chalk will get on your shoe. If it leaves a straight line on your shoe from your toe over the right lacing holes of your shoe, you know you are placing the ball in the right position on your kicking foot as you kick it. This should give the ball an end-over-end flight. If you want to kick a spiral, point the ball a little to the inside (to the left for right-footed kickers and to the right for left-footed kickers).

Follow-through

After the ball has been kicked, let your leg follow through with its swing. Some kickers keep the other foot on the ground during this follow-through. Some kick so high, the other foot leaves the ground. Watch a good punter. His kicking foot usually goes higher than his head during the last part of his follow-through. Your foot and leg should be stretched out and your knee and ankle locked during the follow-through.

Place-kicking

A tee is sometimes used or else the ball is held by another player for kick-offs and for kicking extra

KICKING FROM A TEE: The toe of your kicking foot should strike
the ball in the center of the seam, when it is set right on the tee.
Never kick the laces.

points or field goals, when you have goal posts. For
all place-kicking, the skills which have to be learned
are the same.

Holding the Ball

If no tee is used, the player who holds the ball for
the kicker plays an important part in making a good
kick. He must hold the ball perfectly so the kicker can
kick it properly. He should sit or squat on both feet
with his front foot and leg stretched out and pointing
in the direction of the kick. He stretches out his arms

YOUR ANKLE LOCKS and stays locked as you kick from a tee, right through the follow-through.

and fingers to provide a target for the pass from the Center. When he gets the ball, he stands it on one end, straight up and down. The fingers of his left hand (for a right-footed kicker) should hold the ball firmly on the top until after it is kicked. His other hand should be used to turn the ball as he gets it so that the laces face the direction of the kick. The kicker will not be as accurate if he has to kick the ball on the laces.

Taking Steps

You take the same steps as in punting. As the holder places the ball on the ground for you to kick, you should be back $1\frac{1}{2}$ steps. First, you take a short half step with your right foot, then a full step with your left foot, ending with your left foot almost even with the ball. Then make the kick with your right foot. (If you are left-footed, start the short step with your left foot, etc.)

The Place-kick

The toe of the shoe of your kicking foot should strike exactly in the center of the ball. Don't use the top of your toe . . . bury the end of your toe in the football. Your toe should strike the ball while your ankle and knee are locked stiff. Your ankle *must not* bend. Here your toe *must not* be stretched out as it is in a punt, but must be locked in the standing position.

Keep Your Eye on the Ball

While you are place-kicking, just as in punting, you must not take your eye off the ball. If you look at the spectators, or the opposing linemen rushing at you, or at the spot you intend to kick it, or at anything else, you will not kick the ball straight. Watch the ball until you make the kick. *Don't watch* the ball after you kick it. Watch your toe strike it, but keep your head down looking at the ground.

Follow-through

After your foot has kicked the ball, don't try to stop all your movements. Let your foot and leg continue in the swing, reaching as high as you can with your toe (now outstretched) just as in the punt. Notice that some college and pro football place-kickers end their kick with their foot above their heads. This helps them kick the ball a greater distance.

Practice

You can't be a good kicker without practice. Knowing how is important, but you can't kick well without practice. Even after you learn how to do it and can kick well, you must still practice. It is not always easy because you need a place to practice kicking. A vacant lot, a school playground or a park might be used. The best place, of course, is an actual football field. Two players will do—work with your father or another boy. Get 25 or 30 yards apart and practice kicking to each other—both punting and place-kicking. It would help if you each had a kicking tee. The tee need not be expensive. Plastic kicking tees can be bought in toy stores which will serve your needs very well.

When four kickers practice together, two of you will hold the ball for the two who are kicking, and then change places so that all four get practice kicking. You can make a game out of it and see who makes the longest kicks. You can also see who makes the most accurate kicks. This can be done by kicking along a straight line and see who can make the ball land closest to the line. The number of feet it lands away from the line is subtracted from the distance it is kicked to give you a "score." For example, if you kicked the ball 60 feet, but it landed 10 feet to the right or left of the line, your score would be 50.

Another game you can play while practicing is Kick Goal. In this game, two boys face each other about 25 to 50 yards apart. The object of the game is to get close enough to the other boy's goal line, to kick the ball over it. You start by trying to kick the ball over the other player's head. If you don't kick it far enough he can catch the ball, and kick from that spot. If it goes over his head, and he can't catch it, he has to chase it, then kick it back from the spot where he picks it up. So he has to kick it farther to kick it over your head. You stand where you are. If your opponent fails to reach you with his return kick, you get the ball closer to his goal line.

If the other boy catches the ball on the fly, he gets to take five GIANT steps towards your goal line before he kicks, which brings him closer to your goal line. So, if you can kick it over his head all the time, or catch all his kicks, you can work your way close enough to his goal line. You might be able to kick the ball over his head and over it and earn 6 points. The boy who makes the most points wins.

You can also play this game with two or more boys on a team. You can either punt or place-kick.

Regardless of how you practice, or where, the important thing is to practice, practice, practice, if you want to be a good kicker or punter.

4. THE STANCE

Have you ever noticed how runners in the 100-yard dash on a track team take their places on the starting line? How quickly they get started is important. They must start at the exact moment they hear the starting gun. If they start too late, the other runners will get too far ahead of them and win. If they start too soon, the starter calls them all back and makes them start again. In football, it is very much the same. Nobody can start until the Center snaps the ball.

There is a rule that the team with the football (the "offensive" team) must stand still for 1 second before the Center can snap the ball. If anyone moves, his team gets a penalty. If the players on the scrimmage line—the lineman—start too soon the umpire calls it "offside" and the penalty is 5 yards. If players in the offensive backfield move at all, it is called "backfield in motion" and the penalty is also 5 yards.

The "defensive" team (the team trying to stop the offensive team from scoring), must also obey the rule. It is the same for them, except that the men in the backfield may move before the ball is snapped.

Just as in track, players on a football team must

THE 4-POINT STANCE: From this position, a lineman is ready to make a strong charge. He should look forward, not down.

start quickly and with power. The defensive linemen must charge across the line of scrimmage to push the offensive linemen out of the way and tackle the ball carrier. The offensive linemen must keep them from doing it. If one of them doesn't start soon enough, the player opposite him can push him out of the way easily. How you stand when you are waiting for the ball to be snapped is called the "stance." How you hold your body, where you put your feet, and how you hold your head are all important. There are several different ways to do it. Let's see what they are.

The 4-point Stance

Look at the picture showing the 4-point stance. Can you see why it is called the 4-point stance? The boy has four parts of his body touching the ground—two hands and two feet. This stance is used by the linemen. From this position he can watch everything taking place along the line of scrimmage. If he keeps his head up, he can see the ball, and he can watch the other players when they move, to see what they are doing.

To take this stance, walk up to the scrimmage line and stand, placing your feet about as wide apart as your shoulders. They should not be in an even line. The toe of the foot you are starting forward with should be even with the heel of your other foot. If you are right-handed, your starting foot would be your right foot (your left foot if left-handed).

After you get your feet in the right place, lean forward on both hands. They should also be about as far apart as your feet. How far you lean forward depends on how tall you are, usually about 18 to 24 inches. You can't measure this each time, you have to practice it until you know how far it should be for you. Bend your knees. They can't be stiff because you can't start quickly or jump if your knees are stiff. Bend them so you can't feel the power in your leg muscles. Your back must be straight and your tail must be about as high as your head. If your head is lower than your tail, you can be pushed down on your face. If your tail is lower than your head, you can be pushed backwards to your back. Your arms shouldn't be stiff either. Relax them a little at the elbows and use your knuckles for support, rather than the palms of your hands.

From this position, or stance, you are ready to

4-POINT STANCE (front view): When you want to move forward with power, this is the stance to use.

charge forward very fast to push someone out of the way or keep him from pushing you out of the way.

Notice the position of the shoulders also. Football players use their shoulders rather than their hands to hit, or push other football players. In the 4-point stance, notice how they are held ready to hit. You have to hold your shoulders up and they have to be straight in line with the scrimmage line, so you won't get pushed to one side.

Now practice this stance until you can get into it correctly each time. Take turns with another boy, with one of you watching and the other doing it and

3-POINT STANCE: With this stance, you can move from the line of scrimmage fast and change direction easily.

correct each other. Get your father, mother, or someone else to help you.

Don't use your knees. When you get tired, the first thing you want to do is to kneel down, but don't do it. If you do, you are making it easy for your opponent to charge into you and push you over. When you are on your knees, you can't move quickly either. From the 4-point stance you are ready to "explode" forward with great speed and power. If you are on your knees you can't explode and you become an easy target for the boy who is trying to block you or push you out of the way.

The 3-point Stance

This stance is also used by linemen sometimes. Look at the picture showing the boy using a 3-point stance. Can you see why it is called a 3-point stance? Notice that only one of his hands is touching the ground. He has one arm and hand resting over one leg. When using the 4-point stance, you have lots of power to move straight ahead, but you can't move to the side very well. Using the 3-point stance, you lose some of your power, but you can move to the side easily. Your feet, body, head, and shoulders are all placed and held in the same way as the 4-point stance. When playing on the line, you usually use the 4-point stance. But when playing at End, you may use either the 3-point or the 4-point stance.

CENTER'S STANCE: His weight is not on the ball but on his feet. His body is level and his shoulders face straight ahead. His head is up, so he can see in front.

The Center Stance

The Center on the offensive team must use a very special stance so he can get the ball to the Quarterback and still keep from being pushed on his face. It looks a little like a 4-point stance. Look at the picture. The Center's feet are wider apart than in the other stances because he has to have room between his legs to get the ball through them to the Quarterback.

Now look at his back, shoulders, and head. They

look almost the same as in the 3- or 4-point stance, don't they? However, there is a big difference. The weight of his body is all on his legs and feet. He has no weight on the ball. He is actually holding the ball, even though it is resting on the ground. With his right hand he will move the ball, almost like he was going to pass it, and his left hand will help guide it through his legs. The things you have to remember when using this stance are to keep your legs wide apart, keep your weight on your legs, and do not lean on the ball. In this stance the Center is ready to snap the ball to the Quarterback and charge forward into the player in front of him.

The Backfield Stance

A player in the backfield, either on offense or defense, cannot use the same stance as the linemen. If he used a 3- or 4-point stance, he would be too close to the ground to "see" the play. He has to stand up so he can watch the Quarterback or the ball carrier better, and still make a fast start. Of course, if he is going to run with the ball, he knows exactly where he is going to move. If he is going to block for the ball carrier, he knows too. If he is on defense, he doesn't know what to expect. In any event, the best stance for him to use is the 2-point stance. Look at the picture on page 63.

See why it is called a 2-point stance? He has only two things touching the ground . . . his feet.

A backfield player's feet should be spread apart about as wide as his shoulders to help balance his body. They can be even with each other, or the starting foot in back a little (right foot for right-handed boys and left foot for left-handed boys). He pushes with his back foot and takes the first step with it—just like a sprinter starting a foot race!

In this stance, the backfield player should always be facing the line of scrimmage. Notice also in the picture how his knees are slightly bent and his body is leaning forward. In this position, he is ready to make a fast start. If he is on defense and there is a kick or a pass, he might have to move backwards quickly. His arms are not held on his hips. They hang loosely out in front, ready to be used as needed to knock down a pass or to push a blocker out of the way. So you see, the stance of a man playing defense in the backfield is as important as on offense. He must be ready to move in any direction the moment he knows which way to go.

2-POINT OR BACKFIELD STANCE: From this position you can see all the action on the field and are ready to move in any direction.

5. TACKLING AND BLOCKING

Young football players run a risk of physical injury in a game that includes tackling, so here we will try to reduce the risk and hopefully avoid all possibility of injury. For if there is no tackling, it is not football—it is touch football, quite a different game and one that emphasizes passing rather than running with the ball.

Therefore, before you play a tackling game you must have a rockless grassy field, as described on page 82. Also, each boy must be wearing the full uniform—helmet with face guard, shoulder pads, athletic supporter, mouth guard, and preferably hip pads, as well as padded pants. Sneakers or rubber-soled football shoes should be worn—not cleats.

This type of "Playing with a Football" is actually less dangerous than touch football because it is played with full body protection. On the other hand, the "touch" is often a wild swing which can injure an unprotected boy more than a tackle on a grassy field, when the ball carrier and tackler are both well protected with equipment.

DON'T PLAY A TACKLE GAME unless you have a grassy field and full equipment for each player! Only then are you ready to play this game.

How to Tackle

A tackle can be made only on the ball carrier, and only attempted by a defensive player. A tackle can be made in many ways—by grabbing an arm, a shirt-tail, or a foot. But, these are not good tackles, as the runner can get away too easily. So don't use them. Unless your team tackles well, it will be hard for you to win games.

The best tackle is one that brings the ball carrier quickly to the ground. Although 2 or 3 players often make a tackle together, it is usually made by one player. How do you grab a ball carrier who is running as hard as he can and bring him to the ground? There are three main ways to do it: by a "head-on" tackle, a "side" tackle, or a "behind" tackle. Good players know how to use them all.

The Head-on Tackle

If the ball carrier is coming straight at you, you have to make a head-on tackle to stop him. You have to meet him head-on and bring him down. Grabbing an arm or shirt-tail won't do it. If you make a poor tackle, or miss the ball carrier, he could score a touchdown. First of all, you must move quickly and get close to the ball carrier. You should be about 2 to 3 feet from the ball carrier—close enough to him to make the tackle, and yet far enough away so you

READY TO TACKLE: Arms up at the waist, neck pulled into his shoulder pads, head and eyes up to watch the ball carrier, this tackler is prepared.

can move quickly if the ball carrier suddenly changes direction. If you try to make the tackle too soon, the ball carrier can move out of your way. If you wait too long, he can run over you.

The next thing you must do is to get your body ready. You must be balanced. You can do this by making sure your feet are wide apart—about as wide as your shoulders. Your body should be leaning forward and your arms hanging down naturally in front of you. Your knees should be bent a little so you can move. You can't jump or move quickly if you keep your knees stiff. Try it. Hold your knees stiffly and try to jump without bending them. You can't jump very high or very far, can you? By bending them a little, you are ready to move fast and hard. You must also have your eyes open, and looking at the belt of the ball carrier. If you watch his face, head, or legs, he can use them to fool you, and make you miss the tackle. So don't watch his face or his legs—watch his stomach.

As you get close enough to make the tackle—2 to 3 feet—bring your arms up and charge into the ball carrier. Aim the top of your shoulder for his legs above his knees. Aim your head to one side of his body, preferably the side where he is carrying the ball. Some coaches say that you should aim your head at his stomach. This is not good for boys, as youngsters' neck muscles may not be fully developed and you could get hurt. Even with a helmet you could get hurt. You could also hurt the ball carrier. Wrap your arms

HEAD-ON TACKLE: Put your arms around the ball carrier's legs, keep your head low and near the ball, and your shoulder above his knees.

around his legs just below the knees, and hold them tightly to your chest. Your head, shoulder, and arms should all hit the ball carrier at the same time. You should be driving hard with your feet to push him backwards and to the ground. Try to fall on top of him. You should keep both feet on the ground. If you are standing up straight as you meet him, he will knock you backwards, making you let go of him.

You should never let the ball carrier fall forward if you can possibly help it. Push him back; don't let him push you back. Look at the pictures, showing a boy making a head-on tackle. See how he uses his shoulder? Look also how low he is. You see how he can drive with his legs to push the ball carrier back.

The Side Tackle

There are times when you will not be able to meet the ball carrier head-on. He may try to go around you, or you might overtake him from the side. Then you must make a side tackle. Try to aim your head, neck, and shoulders in front of him. Use your arms to reach around both his legs from the side and pull them together. If you can't get both legs, try to get the one on the farther side from you. Pull his knees together against your chest if you can, and hold them tightly. This makes him lose his balance and fall. Hang on tightly and as you both go to the ground, try to roll over so you will be on top as you stop rolling. Look at the picture on the next page showing a boy making a side tackle.

SIDE TACKLE: Keep your head low and in front of the runner. Try to tackle around the ball carrier's two legs and bring them together against your chest.

The Behind Tackle

At times you will need to make a tackle on the ball carrier from behind. If you are chasing him, it will not be possible for you to get around in front of him or to his side. You must bring him to the ground from behind. You have to aim high and jump on him hard. You don't use your shoulder or head. Try to grab him around the waist or shoulder from behind. Although, in pro football, tackles are made around the neck and head, boys shouldn't do it. What you actually do is to jump on his back with your arms around him and drag him to the ground. If you miss his shoulder, you might be able to grab his legs or a foot and trip him as you fall. You have to keep your eyes open at all times. As you grab him, hold on tightly until you have pulled him to the ground.

Here are some things to keep in mind on all tackles:

■ *Keep your eyes open*—if you can't see you can't tackle. Watch the ball-carrier.

■ *Keep your feet on the ground and drive.* You can't change direction with your feet off the ground.

■ *Keep driving with your legs.* Even after you have your arms around him, keep driving with your legs.

■ *Use your shoulders.* Your shoulders are strong, use them to hit the ball carrier. They are tougher than your head and can hit harder than your head. With your shoulders against his body and your head and neck to his side, you can hold him as in a vice.

SHOULDER BLOCK: Without using your hands, this is how you block the opposing lineman, moving him to your right.

- *Keep your head tucked in*, like a turtle, between your shoulders and still watch what is going on. Don't try to make a tackle standing straight up.
- *Lock your arms tightly around the runner.* Don't let him go.
- *Practice making tackles.* Use a dummy, if you can find one, or make one from a sack filled with old rags and hang it from a tree. If you can't find a dummy, work with one of your friends—tackle each other. Try not to hurt each other. Make tackles on a grassy field on each other "gently." Learn how to make all three kinds of tackles.

How to Block

Without good tackling your team cannot keep the opposing ball carrier from scoring. Without good blocking, your team cannot score. The offensive team blocks to get a defensive player out of the way so he cannot tackle the ball carrier. Good blocking is the most important part of a good offense.

A block has to be made in a special way or your team will be penalized. It is against the rules to use your hands in making a block or use them or your arms as weapons. So a block must be made with the body. If you wrap your arm around a man, it is called "holding," and the penalty is 15 yards, even if you just hang onto his shirt or arm.

There are two main kinds of blocks: the shoulder block and the body block. You should learn how to do them both.

SHOULDER BLOCK (front view): Here you can see how to use your shoulder and keep your head clear. Use your legs to drive and push.

The Shoulder Block

This block is used frequently by a lineman to move an opposing lineman out of the way so the ball carrier can run through the line. It is almost like a head-on tackle, except that you must block without using your hands. You usually start from a 3- or 4-point stance so you get lots of power from your body and legs.

As the ball is snapped, you charge straight forward into the player you are trying to move out of the way. You should aim your head to one side of his body, not the middle of his body. If you are trying to move him to the right, your head should be on the left side of his body as you look at him. If you are trying to move him to the left, your head should be on the right side of his body. Your shoulder should be aimed at his middle—his stomach.

Try to keep under his arms, which he will be using to keep you away from him. As your shoulder hits his stomach, drive hard with your legs to push him out of the way. Don't let him get away from you. Keep right on charging him until he is down or out of the way. Use your shoulder and body, but not your hands. The defensive player can use his hands to push you out of the way, however.

The Body Block

This is sometimes called the "open field block" when it is made by the offensive player who is running "interference," trying to protect the ball carrier as

BODY BLOCK: Move in front of the opposing player and use your side, shoulder, head and arm to block him.

he runs around the end of the scrimmage line, or through it to the goal line. This block is usually the one used against running defensive players (backfield defenders usually) to keep them from getting close enough to the ball carrier to make the tackle. It is much like the side tackle, except that the hands cannot be used.

To body block, you have to be close enough to the runner so that you won't miss him. With the shoulder block you try to drive your opponent back, but with the body block you try to stop him from running. To do it, you throw your body in front of him, with your head, shoulders, and neck across his thighs. Then, keeping your feet, you try to walk like a crab—sideways—keeping him from getting around you. Always push against him. If he moves back, move back with him.

If you let him get away, he can still tackle the runner. You must keep him from going anywhere, but you cannot use your hands. Look at the picture. Can you see how the blocker is keeping his man from getting going without using his hands?

Sometimes two blockers will work as a team to make sure the man is blocked away from a play, or a ball carrier. When they do this, they talk with each other so they know what to do. One blocker will use a shoulder block high on the man's stomach and the other will use a low body block on his legs.

Most boys have a hard time learning to block, because it is hard to block without using hands and keeping both feet on the ground. But it must be done.

PUSH-UPS: Keep your body low and straight. Don't bend your neck. Touch the grass with your nose, then push your body back up with your arms alone. You can do 15 to 20 of these each day.

WINDMILL: Touch your right toe with your left hand then your left toe with your right hand. Keep your knees stiff and come back to standing position in between. You can do 20 to 25 of these each day.

If you try to hold a player with your hands, the penalty is a big one—15 yards! So learn how to do it right. This takes a lot of practice. If you can find a tackling dummy, you can use it to practice shoulder blocking. You might make one from a big sack filled with rags. Hang it up from a cross-bar, in front of you, and face it while kneeling. Then charge it, letting your face go to one side of it as you hit it with your shoulder. Keep low, so you can get all the power your legs and back can give. As your shoulder strikes the dummy, your head and eyes should be looking up. This helps you squeeze the dummy. You should try to pinch the dummy between your shoulder and your head. Practice going to the left and the right of the dummy.

Practicing with a friend is also good when you are learning to body block. Change places so that each of you takes a turn being the blocker. See who can do it the best. When you are the blocker, try to keep the other boy from getting around you. When you are the other boy, try to get away from the blocker. Push him to the ground. You might make a game out of it by keeping score to see who is the best. Each time you win you get a point. The first to get 10 points wins the game.

As you will see, a good blocker needs strong shoulders and neck muscles. Do exercises each day which will help build good neck and shoulder muscles. Don't forget the leg and back muscles either. Do some exercises to make these strong also. These same exercises will help you build muscles for making

SIT-UPS: Have a friend hold your ankles, and place your hands on top of or behind your head. Lie down and lift your body up from the hips until your elbows touch your knees. Do this 20 to 25 times. (Indoors, hook your shoes under a couch.)

PULL-UP OR CHIN-UP: If no bar is available, use a sturdy tree limb. With your feet off the ground, pull your chin up even with the bar, then lower yourself. With practice, you can do this 8 times or more.

good tackles. The pictures show some good ones you can do. Practice some each day, and keep up a real desire to have good muscles. If you get into the habit of doing these for 10 to 15 minutes at the same time each day, you could build some strong muscles. Choose a time when you can do them easily—when you get up in the morning, or before you go to bed at night—and do them faithfully. Good football players have to be strong.

6. RULES OF THIS GAME

Football teams use eleven men—seven on the line of scrimmage and four in the backfield. When you play football in the back yard, vacant lot, in the park, or on the school grounds, you probably won't have this many players, but you can still play football and have fun. You might have to change the rules a little, but you can use most of them.

First of all, mark off the field. Stay off paved streets and parking areas—there is too much danger of getting hurt. An empty grassy lot or grassy playground that is free of rocks is best. Measure it by walking along the sides and ends to see how many steps long and wide it is. Try to find a place at least 50 steps long and 20 to 25 steps wide. Mark the four corners some way—use a tree or bush. You can use a coat, cap, or shirt for corner markers also.

You probably will not be able to have a goal post, but you can get along without it. You won't need an end zone either. Use the end of the field you have marked out as a goal line. Mark a line across the field at both ends for the goal line, using a shirt, coat or stick. Be sure everybody knows where the line is. Also mark the center of the field in some way. Look at the way we have marked the field in the illustration.

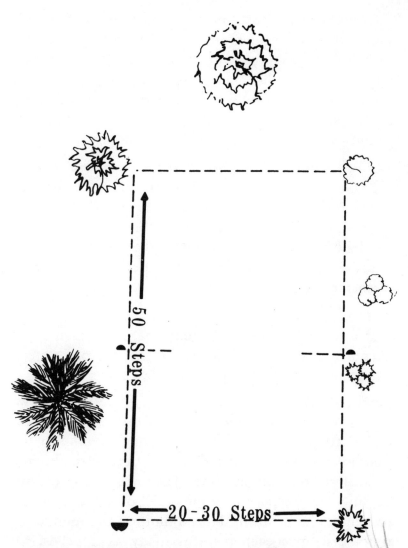

50 Steps

20-30 Steps

A GRASSY FIELD: A playing area of about 30 by 50 steps is fine. Use trees, shrubs and rocks (or else clothing) to mark the corners.

While you can use most of the rules of football, you will need to make up 12 special commandments for your field, and for your game. Here are some which will work if you have no more than 4, 5 or 6 men on each team. If you follow these rules, you won't need an umpire, but if an adult is with you, or you can round one up, invite him to be the umpire.

1. *Each team can keep the ball for only four downs.*
In other words, even if a team moves the ball 10 yards, it does not get a first down again. With a small field, this rule will probably work better than the real football rule. It will also make the game more fun because each team will have more chances to be the offensive team.

2. *Punts on 4th down.*
If a punt goes over the goal line, the ball may be caught and run out, or it can be brought out 5 steps from the goal line and put into play there.

3. *No team is allowed to stall the ball between plays.*
You won't have a clock and a timer, so each team will need to be fair about how long to take in the huddle and in time-outs. You need time in the huddle to call plays, and at times you will need to stop playing, but keep your "time-outs" only long enough to handle the problem. Put no limit on the number of time-outs—give each team as many as it needs. Of course, a time-out can only be called after a play is completed—not while it is taking place.

4. *All forward passes must be from behind the line of scrimmage, and not after the ball crosses it.*

This rule is the same as in real football. After the ball crosses the line of scrimmage, it may be passed, but only backwards or to the side. A pass can be thrown across the field, but it can't go toward the goal line—not even a little bit. Without an umpire or referee, you all need to be fair about this. The penalty would be loss of that down.

5. *No offside allowed.*

After the offensive linemen take their stance, no offensive player may move for at least one second before the ball is snapped, except one. One Back of the offensive team may move, but he can't move forward. He can move toward the sideline or toward the rear. Defensive players can move about on or behind the line but may not cross it. Also, no one may jump over the line of scrimmage before the ball is snapped. The offside penalty for the offense is a loss of the down. If the defense is offside, the offense gets an extra down.

6. *Anyone can catch a pass.*

In real football only certain men can be pass receivers—the Backfield players and the Ends. But in this game, everyone can be a pass receiver. You don't have so many players and more boys will have a chance to handle the ball.

7. *Players must not use their hands, fists, arms, or feet as weapons to hurt another player.*

This is the same rule as real football. It won't be

fun if boys get into fights or injure each other. So don't grab a defensive player with your hands, don't hit him with your arms, elbows, fists or feet, and trip him. Block him, instead, with a good block as described in Chapter 5. The penalty for violation is loss of down. Boys who get into fights should be removed from the game.

8. *Offensive men can block, but not tackle.*

The block must be made from the front or side, not from the rear. There is a danger in illegal blocks— hurting a player who is not expecting to be blocked and cannot defend himself. Blockers must also keep their feet on the ground. The penalty for violation is the loss of the down.

9. *Defensive men can tackle and block.*

Tackles should be made as described in Chapter 5, and blocks also. The penalty for an illegal tackle or block is the loss of the down.

10. *Kick-offs are to be made from the goal line.*

This is because the playing field is small, and because of Rule 1.

11. *Field goals.*

Field goal attempts will count if the ball goes over the goal line, unless it is caught. Defensive teams may not have anyone back of the goal line until the ball is kicked. If the ball is caught on a field goal attempt, it may either be "grounded" and brought out 5 steps from the goal line to be put into play, or it may be run back.

12. *The point after touchdown.*

The point can be made by running or by kicking. The ball should be brought out 5 steps from the goal line to make the try for the extra point. If it is kicked over the goal line, the point is good *unless the ball is caught.* If it is caught, the point is no good and the team making the touchdown will kick off to the other team.

7. PLAYING OFFENSE

How the Linemen Play

In our game, the linemen have two important jobs to do—to protect the ball carrier (or the kicker or punter), and to get through the line to catch a pass. In real football, the Ends are the only linemen who can catch passes, but in our game the Center and any offensive player can also catch passes. This makes the game more fun for boys. Let's see how to do it.

The players on the offensive line must take a 3- or 4-point stance and be ready to move as soon as the ball is snapped. If it is going to be a running play, they must block the defensive players out of the way so as to make a hole in the scrimmage line for the ball carrier to go through. They need to know when and how to make a head-on block, and when to make a body block. They must also remember that they cannot use their hands or arms or it would be called "tackling" and the rules say that offensive men cannot tackle. So they have to use their bodies to block, just as explained in Chapter 5.

The offensive linemen learn from the huddle where the ball carrier is going, so they can block the defensive players out of the way. Suppose you are the Center and the ball carrier is to run in the hole between you and player on your right. Which way will you block the defensive player? You must block away from the ball, so you block to the left in this case. The player on your right blocks to the right. This makes a hole in the scrimmage line for the ball carrier to go through. In this case you might make a body block to keep the defensive player from getting around you or over you before the ball carrier gets through the hole.

If the ball carrier is to go around the End, the whole line needs to block the defensive players away from that side, using head-on or body blocks. If you are playing End, and are to catch a pass, how will you block? You probably will not use the body block, because you have to get around the defensive player so you can get the pass. A head-on block is the one to use. As you come in contact with the defensive player, you block him, or push him out of the way with your shoulders and rolled-up arms. You hold him back just long enough to make him think the play is going to be a running play, and give the passer a little more time. Then you go around him and run fast to the place where you are to catch the pass. The other linemen need to know what you are going to do so they can block the defensive players and keep them from rushing the passer.

How the Backfield Plays

Offensive players in the backfield should always take a 2- or 3-point stance so they can start fast and block for the ball carrier or the punter. If there are only two in your backfield, one will be the ball carrier and the other needs to be his blocker to keep him from being tackled. If the ball carrier is to try to run around the end of the scrimmage line, the other player in the backfield runs along with him and keeps between him and the line of scrimmage to block any defensive player who might get through the line. If the ball carrier is to run through the line of scrimmage, the play might be planned for one backfield player to run through the hole in the line first, to block for the ball carrier who closely follows him.

If the Quarterback is to throw a pass to the End, the other players in the backfield need to block for him to keep the defensive players from rushing him.

When a team has to punt, the kicker must have enough time to get the punt away. So, on punt plays, the kicker plays back from the line of scrimmage 5 or 6 yards and the other player in the backfield blocks for him. The players on the line must block, too, then charge downfield to rush the player who catches the punt. As soon as the punt or kick is made, the offensive team becomes the defensive team so they can tackle the punt receiver. However, they must allow him to catch the ball first before touching him. Then you should tackle the ball carrier rather than block him.

The Quarterback can either play close to the Center, or take his place farther back. When the backfield players play close to the Center and the line of scrimmage, they can make runs into the line quicker, but there is less time to throw passes. When backfield players play back, they have more time to throw passes, but it would take them longer to get into the line on running plays. Good Quarterbacks can play close to the Center and still throw passes, but they must be able to "backpedal"—run backwards—to "set up" and to give the pass receivers time to get through the line, and to have more time to throw a good pass.

Playing close to the Center is usually the best way, because it keeps the defensive team guessing what the play is going to be. Your opponents won't know whether the play is coming through the line or whether the Quarterback is going to backpedal and pass. He might even backpedal to fake a pass, then run with the ball or hand it off to his Running Back to pass or to run the ball. To have a good offense, you need to keep the defense guessing. You need to make the other team think you are going to do one thing and then do something else.

Calling Signals

In the huddle you decide at what signal the ball is going to be snapped by the Center. Almost any word or number can be used as long as it is short and easily heard. Don't use two words or numbers that sound the same. For example, don't use "Four" and "More," because they sound the same. Your team must be able to tell when the right word or number is going to be given, so use what is called a "series" signal. The series signal contains at least three words or numbers. The first word or number tells the team to get ready or to get set. The ball then is snapped on the third word or number, which is called the "key."

Here is an example. In the huddle, the Quarterback tells the team that the signal will be "Down-on-Two." This means that after "Down," the ball will be snapped on the second word or number he says after it. So, as he takes his place, the Quarterback looks around to see that all his players are ready. Then he says "Down" and they all take their stance. Then he yells out the first number or letter, which might be "Blue" or "Three" or anything. The team now knows that the next number or letter will be the key and the ball will be snapped. This is how the signal might be called: "Down! . . . Blue! . . . Six!" and the ball will be snapped when he says: "Six!"

Let's take another example. The Quarterback might give the following signal in the huddle: "Down-on-One." This signal means a quick snap, because the first word or number after "Down" will be the key and the ball will be snapped when he says: "One!"

Let's try another one. Suppose the Quarterback tells the huddle the signal will be: "Set-on-Three." What does he mean? He is saying that when he wants the players to take their stance, he will yell "Set!"

He will follow by yelling three numbers or words, and the key will be the third one. So he might yell "Set—Sky—Blue—One!" The key would be "One" and the ball would be snapped then.

Usually it is not good to use more than three words before the key, because members of the offensive team might not count correctly, and charge before the key was given. So keep the signals short and keep them simple.

The Quarterback needs to yell all words or numbers loudly and clearly so that everybody on the team can hear them. Yell them slowly to give your teammates time to count them correctly. Pause a short time between each word or number, with the pauses all the same length. Practice by playing that you are the Quarterback, and huddle and yell some signals with your friends.

In real football games, the teams all have their own special way of calling signals, because their coaches want them to do certain things. The important thing to remember, no matter what your system, is that all players on your team must understand the signal and all move at the same time when the ball is snapped.

The Formation

How your team lines up on the field ready for the ball to be snapped is called a "Formation." The formation you use depends upon the number of players on your team. If you only have 4 players, the formation will be different than when you have 5 or 6

2-2 PLAN: With a 4-man team, the formation looks like this.

players on a team. Each formation can also be changed to keep the defensive team guessing. Let's take some examples using a 4-man team.

The 2-2 Plan

You can put 2 players on the scrimmage line with 2 in the backfield. In this formation, one lineman needs to be the Center, or the players might take turns being Center. This would give each a chance to play in both places.

One of the backfield would be the Quarterback and the other the Running Back. These boys could also take turns playing Quarterback. This would be a good plan to use also, because it makes it harder for the defensive team to guess who the ball carrier or passer is going to be. The Quarterback might be the ball carrier and use the Running Back as a blocker to help him get around or through the line of scrimmage. Or the Running Back might be the ball carrier and use the Quarterback as a blocker. Either one might get the ball and hand it off or pass it to the other one. The Quarterback could play close to the Center for quick plays through the line or he could play back a little to keep the defensive team guessing.

One bad thing about this plan is that there are only 2 players on the scrimmage line to do the blocking. If the defensive team decides to use 3 players on the scrimmage line, one of them could easily crash through and mess up the play. Another point is that you would not have as many pass receivers to go downfield for a pass.

The 3-1 Plan

With a 4-man team, try using 3 players on the scrimmage line. The one in the middle is the Center, and the others are Ends. With this plan you have only one man in the backfield—the Quarterback. But you have 2 Ends, and either one can be a pass receiver. You keep the defense guessing by mixing pass plays with running plays—having the Quarterback as the ball carrier, going through the line or around it, or passing to one of the Ends. The Quarterback can also fake a run through the line and pass to an End. Or he might fake a pass and run through the line.

SINGLE WING FORMATION with a 4-man team.

The bad thing about this formation is that the defense knows who is going to carry or throw the ball.

To keep the defensive team guessing, you might use a variation of the 2-2. Line up with 2 players on the scrimmage line, and 2 in the backfield. Have them all stand in their places with the Quarterback standing close to the Center. This would make the defensive team think you were going to use a 2-2 formation. Then as the quarterback yells "Down!" or "Set!", the team would shift to a 3-1 formation. The men on the line would shift, or change positions. The Quarterback would become the Center, and the Running Back would become the Quarterback. In our game, this shift would not be against the rules if the linemen

SINGLE WING with a 5-man team.

didn't take their stance before the shift was made. They would all need to be standing straight up at the beginning and then take their stance on the "Down" or "Set" call and remain there at least one second before the ball was snapped.

So you see, there are lots of different plays you could try, even with only 4 men on your team.

If you have enough players for 5 on a team, there are many, many more different formations and plays to use. Let's look at a few.

The Single Wing

With 4 players you can put 2 on the line, play the Quarterback deep, and have the Running Back off to one side. This is a good punt formation.

"I" FORMATION with a 4-man team.

With 5 players you can use 3 on the line—a Center and 2 Ends. This leaves you 2 in the backfield—a Quarterback and a Running Back. If the 2 players in the backfield line up with the Quarterback behind the Center and the Running Back off to the side, the Running Back would be the Single Wing or Wing Back, either on the right or the left. From this formation, you can use about the same type of running plays as with a 4-man team and a 2-man backfield. Either the Quarterback or the Running Back can carry or pass the ball. Either of the Ends can be pass receivers. The Quarterback or the Running Back can fake a run through the line and then pass to the other, or pass to one of the Ends.

"I" FORMATION with a 5-man team.

The "I" Formation

When the Running Back lines up right behind the Quarterback, it is called the "I" formation because if you drew a line through the Quarterback and the Running Back, it would look like the letter "I." You run exactly the same plays as you use with the Single Wing formation. You can shift from the "I" formation to the Single Wing just before the ball is snapped. Or you can run your plays from the "I" formation. The main reason for using the "I" is to keep the defensive team guessing what play you are going to use.

"T" FORMATION with a 5-man team and the QB in the backfield. Either the Quarterback or the Running Back can get the snap from the Center.

The "T" Formation

When the 2 players in the backfield line up side by side with each other, an even distance back from the line of scrimmage, it is called a "T" formation. If you were to draw a line straight back from the Center to where the men in the backfield are lined up, then another line through both of them, the lines would look like the letter "T." The main reason for using the "T" formation is to keep the defensive team guessing.

You can run a play either to the left or right and the defensive team won't know, until it starts, which side to defend. It is a good formation to use for "quick-kick" punting before the fourth down. Running plays can be planned just like those of the Single Wing. You can fake a run, then pass. Or you can fake a pass, then run.

In the "T" formation you have more time to pass or get the running play started, but it takes longer to work the plays. This gives the defensive team a better chance to guess what you are going to do. You could line up in a "T," then shift to a Single Wing or an "I" before the ball is snapped. Either one of the backfield men can be the Quarterback. Either one can run the ball or pass it.

Some Running Plays

In these plays, either the Quarterback or the Running Back is the ball carrier. When the Quarterback carries the ball we could call the plays "Q" plays. When the Running Back carries the ball, we could call them "B" plays. Let's look at them.

The Quarterback or "Q" Plays

The best known of all the "Q" running plays is called the "Quarterback Sneak." We could also call this the "Q-C" play because it goes over the Center. It can start from any formation where the Quarterback plays close to the Center. When the ball is snapped, the Center charges into the player opposite in the scrimmage line and the Quarterback follows him through the hole he opens up. The other player (or players) on the line must also charge and block away from the ball. The Running Back helps by

QUARTERBACK CRASHING through the line with the blockers opening a hole. The backfield player should be faking.

fooling the other team into thinking he has the ball and is running with it. In the huddle when the Quarterback calls the play he could say "Quarterback Sneak" or just simply, "Q-C."

The Quarterback Dive

In this play, the whole offensive team must know exactly where the Quarterback is going to rush or dive into the line. Some coaches make it easier for their players by giving numbers to the spaces between the players on the line. Let's see how it works. Numbers go from left-to-right. With a 3-man line, start at the left side and call the space off the end of the line, number "1"; the space between the End and the Center, space number "2"; the space between the Center and the other End, space number "3"; and the space off the other side of the line would be space number "4." Now the Quarterback can tell his team

Q-3 PLAY: The Quarterback is carrying the ball through space number 3 in the line. The linemen are blocking away from the ball carrier.

where he will try to get through the line. Look at the top photo. The Quarterback has called for a "Q-3" play, and he will try to get through the line by crashing or diving through space number 3. The linemen on each side of space number 3 know that they have to block away from the ball—the End blocks to his right and the Center to his left.

END RUN: The QB is running the ball through space number 4, around the end of the scrimmage line. (With a 3-man line this would be space number 3.)

The End Run

If the Quarterback calls for play "Q-4," where will he try to crash through the line? He will try to go around Right End, won't he? The offensive Right End needs to block to the left—away from the ball so the Quarterback can get around the defensive End. The other linemen need to block straight ahead or to the left to keep the other defensive players from running toward the Quarterback to tackle him. The Running Back needs to run along with the Quarterback to help with the blocking also. He helps most by keeping between the Quarterback and the defensive players to block them out of the way so the Quarterback can run.

The Quarterback Option or the "Q-O" Play

The word "option" is just another word for choice or decide. After the Quarterback gets the ball and starts to run towards the end of the scrimmage line he can choose between continuing to run with the ball or tossing it to the Running Back and letting him run with it. You must have seen this many times in football games. A defensive lineman gets through the line and tackles the Quarterback, but before the Quarterback's knees touch the ground, he tosses the ball backwards or sideways to the Running Back, who then runs with the ball around the scrimmage line. The Quarterback has another option. If a hole opens up in the line of scrimmage, he can choose to turn into the line and run through the hole.

In the huddle, the Quarterback calls for the play

QB OPTION: The Quarterback here-has a choice. He can run or hand off or toss the ball to the Running Back who moves alongside him.

"Q-O Left," and everybody on his team knows that he is going to run the option play to the left side of the line. The linemen on the left side will block for him and the Running Back will run along with him, a little to his left so he can get the ball when the Quarterback tosses it. If the Quarterback calls for a "Q-O Right" in the huddle, which way would he run the option play? Which way would the linemen block? Which way would the Running Back go?

The Running Back or "B" Plays

In "B" plays, the Running Back carries the ball. In a Single Wing or an "I" formation, the Quarterback

B-PLAY: Here the Quarter-back turns and hands off to the Running Back who goes through the line.

usually plays close to the Center and gets the ball as it is snapped. So if the Quarterback calls for a "B" play, the Running Back must get the ball from the Quarterback in a hand-off (see pages 25–31).

In the huddle, the Quarterback might call for a "B-3" play. If you are the Running Back, where will you go? You run towards space number 3 in the line, and get the ball from the Quarterback as you go by him. The linemen on either side of space number 3 block away from the ball to make a hole for you, and

B-1 PLAY: The Running Back has received the ball from the Quarterback. His teammates are blocking for him—to the right, so he can run around the left end.

if everything goes well, you run through the hole in the line, and maybe for a touchdown!

If the Quarterback called for a "B-1" play, where will you go if you are the Running Back? You run toward the left end (space number 1). The players on your line need to block for you to keep the defensive players from tackling you. In a "T" formation, the Running Back gets the ball on a direct pass from the Center himself and there is no need for a hand-off.

These plays take lots of practice. The Quarterback must make a good hand-off to you, the Running

Back. If he or you should drop it for a fumble, the other team might get the ball. (See page 42, Loose Balls.) You need to learn just where to stand, and which way to go so you can make the hand-off easy for the Quarterback.

Some Passing Plays

Passes are the easiest way to move the ball down the field, but they don't always work. You need to have a good passer and a good receiver or the defensive team can intercept the ball and make a touchdown. The defensive team has a much better chance of getting the ball away from you in passing plays than they do in running plays.

Passes can be made from any formation, but you have to remember a few things about passes:

■ they cannot be thrown forward after the passer crosses the line of scrimmage

■ the passer must be protected

■ you must have someone to catch the pass.

In real football, only certain men may catch the passes—the Ends and the backfield men. But in our game, the rule is that any player may catch passes. This includes the Center as well as the Ends. There are many different kinds of passes, but let's look at one or two of the most common types.

The "Hook" Pass

In this pass the Ends, who are usually the receivers, somehow get over the line of scrimmage, and then turn back quickly toward the center of the field behind

HOOK PASS:
The End rushes past his opposing End and turns to catch a quick pass, soon after crossing the scrimmage line.

the line of scrimmage and in front of the defensive men in the backfield. This quick turn is the "hook." To make this work well, the End who will be the pass receiver must get around or through the line of scrimmage very quickly, either by side-stepping or faking the opposing End. If he gets blocked out or held up on the scrimmage line, he will not be able to get to the right place in time to catch the pass and the Quarterback will have to do something else with the ball. The other linemen must block to help the intended receiver get by the defensive linemen, and also to keep them from crashing over the scrimmage line to rush the passer. This pass is usually a short one and is good to use for short gains. Sometimes if the pass receiver is a good open-field runner, he can get away from the defensive men, and go all the way for a touchdown.

If the defensive team uses 3 men on the line of scrimmage with a 4-man team to stop running plays, there would then be only one player in the backfield to defend against the pass. Then, if the receiver catches the pass, he has a good chance to go all the way to the goal line.

The hook pass is best for Ends, because they can get in the right place to catch the ball quicker and easier than any other players on the team. Both of them can charge around the scrimmage line, and the defensive team won't know which one is the receiver until it's too late to stop him. The other End can become a blocker for the receiver so he can run to the goal line.

The "Out" Pass

The receiver gets through the line, or around it, and goes straight down the field, then suddenly turns and runs OUT to the nearest sideline and catches the pass. He must know where the Quarterback will try to throw the ball, so he can be there to get it. The receiver might make it look like he is going to catch this pass while running. In fact, he should try to catch it over his shoulder—the one nearest the sideline—and keep on running right down the sideline.

OUT PASS:
The End
rushes over the
scrimmage line
and into the
opposing
backfield, then
turns toward
the sideline to
receive the
pass.

The TD or "Bomb" Pass

With this long pass to the goal line, the receiver must be able to get through the scrimmage line fast and run down the field very quickly. He must know where the Quarterback will try to throw the ball and then be there when it arrives. Many times when the defensive players see this pass coming, they will move back from the scrimmage line. This gives the Quarterback a chance to run the ball for a good gain. This is exactly what the Quarterback should do if his pass receiver can't get down the field fast enough, or if too many defenders are around him.

The Screen Pass

Here the passer backpedals and waits until there is a "screen" of defensive men and his own blockers in front of him. Then he just tosses the ball over them to his receiver, who hasn't even crossed the scrimmage line. When the receiver catches the ball, there may be no defensive players around him, and he can run through the opposing backfield, possibly to the goal line. To make it work right, the blockers need to allow the defensive players to think they are going to get to the passer, and pedal back with them. Then at the right moment, they block, or trap them, not letting them get to the passer. The receiver just loafs around the scrimmage line until he takes the short pass. The passer moves back and back to make it look like he is going to get thrown for a loss. This fakes the defenders into the trap.

General Suggestions

What you have just read are but a few of the many plays you might plan. See if you can plan some of your own, following the rules given in Chapter 6. To help you make them work better, here are some general suggestions:

1. *Mix up your plays.* If you use a Q-C play all the time, the defensive team would soon catch on and be ready to stop it. So mix up your plays, and make the defensive team guess what you are going to do next.

QB FAKE: An unusual play that sometimes works. The Quarterback fakes to the Back who goes into the line as if he had the ball. The QB then follows him through.

If they think you are getting ready to use a running play, fool them—use a pass play. Try a hand-off play; then try something else. It is part of the game to keep the defense guessing.

2. *Always block away from the ball.* Every player should know and remember what he is to do on every play. He must know which way the ball carrier is planning to go so he can help him. The runner can go nowhere if he doesn't have good blocking. If the ball carrier is going to go through the line between the Center and the Right End, he has to have a hole made for him. The Center blocks to his left and the Right

End blocks to his right—away from the ball. If they block toward the ball, they will not make a hole for the ball carrier. They would plug up the hole rather than make it bigger.

3. *Use clear signals*. Use any words or numbers as a signal to start the play, but keep them short and clear. Don't use two words or numbers that sound the same. If numbers, use either the second or third number the Quarterback calls as the starting signal. He might yell "6-8-7" and the play would begin on "7." If this system is used, it should be decided in the huddle each time to keep the defense guessing.

Flag Football

At times, it might not be good to play tackle football. It's okay to tackle when you have all young boys on each time, with full uniforms, because it is unlikely that you will play rough enough to hurt each other seriously. But if you have big boys and little boys playing together, or if you have all big and older boys, they might hurt each other if they don't have protective equipment—helmets with face masks, shoulder pads and hip pads. Still, if you have a nice soft grassy place to play, but not enough equipment, you can play a form of football—"Flag football"— and you can have almost as much fun. You use all the rules as in Chapter 6 except that you don't tackle. Each boy has a "flag" in a rear pocket, or tucked under his belt in the rear. Instead of tackling the ball carrier, you grab his flag and throw it to the ground

FLAG FOOTBALL: See the flags in their pockets? This is a 4-man team with the QB working close to the Center.

right where you grabbed it. This marks the spot where the next down begins.

You can buy flags especially made for flag football. They have special belts made to hold the special flags. But flags can be made from almost anything. An old sock is good. Strips of cloth about 2 inches wide and 1 foot long will also work. Both teams should have the same kind of flags and wear them the same way—in the right or left rear pocket or under the belt in back. It makes little difference where, as long as both teams use the same position for the flag.

8. PLAYING DEFENSE

Some coaches feel that defense is the most important part of football. If the defense is not good, or if individual men on defense do not do their jobs well, the other team will score. But, if the defense is good enough, the other team *can't* score and can't win. Yet, not many people watch the defensive team. They watch the offensive team, mostly the Quarterback or the ball carrier.

It takes years of practice and experience to be able to play good defensive football. The professionals who play a good defense are proud of their ability to keep the other team from scoring, and are as valuable as players in any position. They have to be *better* than the opposing players on offense.

A good Quarterback has to study the defense of the other team and try to discover its weaknesses, the weaknesses of individual players, and the weaknesses of the team as a whole. He tries to plan good plays that will work well against those weaknesses. Have you ever noticed how a Quarterback in a pro game will call a play to test a new defensive player who has just entered the game? The new player may not be as good as the one he replaced, or he might not be "warmed up" enough. Other times, if the Quarterback thinks a defensive player is tired, he will call for a play to test him. Or if the Quarterback feels the other team is tired or weak in certain positions, or some of its players have not been training well, he will use plays to test their strength and desire to play football.

Rules for Defense

In playing football with 4 or 5 men on each team, you will be using most of the rules for regular football, but some are different. Here they are:

1. *You can't pile on.*

Most of the time it only takes one boy to make the tackle. Sometimes more boys will tackle the same runner. This is just good football. The idea is to stop the runner as soon as possible. Any runner must expect to be tackled, but it is not fair, and is against the rules, to jump on him *after* he is down. When a runner goes to his knees, try very hard to keep from jumping or falling on him. Any boy who does this on purpose should be sent from the field.

2. *Hitting with fists and arms or kicking with feet or knees is not allowed.*

The football field is not a fighting ring. Go someplace else to fight. You can't have fun playing football if someone wants to fight. It ruins the game and causes injuries. This is why anyone who wants to fight in football has to be sent from the field as a penalty. Defensive men must not double up their fists when they are playing. It's too easy to hit someone accidentally. You should play with your hands open.

3. *You cannot cross the line of scrimmage until the ball is snapped.*

On defense, you can move wherever you want, before or during the time the ball is snapped from the Center, except across the scrimmage line. If any part of your body crosses the scrimmage line while the ball is being snapped, you are offside. If you cross the scrimmage line and can't get back before the ball is snapped, you are still offside. In regular football, the penalty is 5 yards, but in our game the offense gets an extra down.

4. *A block or tackle must not be made on a kicker.*

You may block the ball as it is kicked, but you can't touch the kicker while he is kicking the ball because he cannot defend himself. He can be tackled or blocked before he starts to kick, but once he starts to kick, you can't touch him. The penalty is an extra down for the offense.

5. *You cannot use your hands to hold anyone except the ball carrier.*

Only when you tackle the ball carrier, may you use your hands. You cannot use your hands to hold any other player, whether by his clothing, or by your arms or legs or by trapping him. You have to stop him by pushing him, or getting your body in his way.

Rules for Defense ◎ **119**

6. Tackling about the head or around the neck is not allowed.

This is allowed in regular football, but in our game it can be too dangerous.

A team that plays good defense must have a plan. But to make that plan work, each man on the team has to know the plan and know how to help his teammates. It takes a whole team to stop a whole team. As a member of a team, you must do your job well, because the whole team is depending on you.

Let's see how you play defense as an individual.

The Linemen

The players in the line are the ones who must meet the attack first. They are the "first line of defense." If they all do their jobs well, the rest of the team doesn't have much to do. The linemen should be the strongest players on the team. In a running play, they have to push aside the blockers and stop the runner if they can. In a pass play, they must try to rush the passer or knock the ball down. Here is how they do it.

Charging

When the ball is snapped, the first thing you, as defensive lineman, must do is to move forward quickly and push the player opposite you out of the way. This is called "charging" or sometimes "crashing." The player opposite you will be trying to stop your charge without using his hands—he will be blocking. So you have to keep from being blocked as you make your charge.

Your charge has to be timed just right. If made too soon—before the ball is snapped—it is called offside! If you charge too late, you can be blocked out of the way and the ball carrier can get through the line right past you.

Sometimes two men will try to block you out of the way. When this happens, it means that the ball carrier might be coming right toward you. Don't try to charge them both. Charge the one who is between you and the ball carrier. This might be the player in front of you or the one at the side. You can't use your hands to hold him back, but you can use your hands, arms, and body to push him out of the way. Try to push him back, and keep him away from you. If you can push him to the ground and get away from him, you can then make the tackle to stop the ball carrier.

How do you make a charge? Let's start from the beginning—before the ball is snapped.

The Shoulder Charge. One of the best charges to make, the shoulder charge, is very much like the shoulder block. You should keep low and explode or leap forward with all your power. Try to hit the man in front of you with your shoulder somewhere below his shoulders and drive him back. You should use your right shoulder if your right foot is the one in back when you take your stance. Use your left shoulder if your left foot is the one in back. The back foot moves forward as you charge. As your shoulder hits him, try to lift him up and push him backward. This will take away all his power and keep him from making a good block on you.

The Arm Charge. Some players like to use their arms to push the man out of the way. You can use one arm or both arms. When you use two arms, try to hit the other player on both his shoulders with the heels of your hands—not your fists. Try to push him off to the side and keep him away from you. When you use one arm, bring your arm up in front of you and under his arms, hitting him on the chest or just under his chest. Push or "drive" with your legs as hard as you can and move him back or out of your way, and then go toward the ball.

The Fake. You might try using a quick step to the right or to the left to fake the other player out of position, then quickly charge him from the side. Don't do this too often as he might catch on to what you are doing, and can take advantage of you when you are off-balance.

The Mouse-Trap or "Trap." Many times you will be allowed to think you can make a quick and easy tackle on the ball carrier as you charge through the line, but it's a trap. The offensive linemen don't try very hard to stop you—they back up and let you charge right over the scrimmage line. Then they "trap" you with a good block and the ball carrier goes zipping right through the hole you left! If you find yourself moving into a trap, forget about trying to tackle the ball carrier. Stop quickly and drop to your hands and feet as in a 3- or 4-point stance to make it harder for the offensive linemen to make a good block on you. In this position, you are ready to make a new charge. Then push off your opponents with your hands (not your fists) and try to keep them from moving you away from the area you are ēxpected to defend.

On Punts. A lineman also has to be a blocker and should be able to make at least two blocks. You should block the offensive man nearest you with a good block, pushing him to the ground if possible. Then you should see where your punt returner is going, and be ready to block for him as he comes upfield. But your first and most important job is to make the first block a good one. If you don't do this, your runner won't get far enough up the field to need a second blocker. If you miss your block, your opposing lineman will be able to get to the ball carrier and tackle him.

A good defensive lineman knows what to do when charging. He tries to keep the players on the other team guessing what he is going to use next. If he makes the same moves all the time, the other players can figure out ways to keep him blocked. You should practice with someone until you know how to make all the right moves.

The Ends

The Ends have the job of keeping the ball carrier from going around the end of the scrimmage line on running plays. Most of the time the ball carrier will have someone else running along with him as a blocker or as interference. If he has no blocker, you, as End, should make the tackle. But if he does have a blocker, you must push the blocker out of the way so someone else can make the tackle.

On running plays through the scrimmage line, your job is pretty much the same. Try to tackle the runner if you can, but your first job is to charge into the line and keep from being pushed out of the way by a blocker. Try to stop the play from coming through the line.

On pass plays, you must not let a receiver get behind you. Try to catch the ball yourself, if you can. If not, try to knock it down so the receiver can't catch it. If you can't do any of these things, and the receiver catches the ball, you should try to tackle him and bring him to the ground before he goes very far.

The Backfield

In playing in the backfield on defense, you must be ready to move fast in the right direction. You cannot charge with the linemen. You have to wait until the linemen charge, because you need to know which way the play is going. If you charge into the middle of the line, or to one side, the ball carrier might change his direction and run away from you. However, you can't wait too long or the ball carrier might be able to get around you. So, a backfield defensive player must be able to read the play quickly and accurately and then move very fast to stop the play. The general rule is to watch for a pass first, then charge the line.

In playing the backfield on defense you must also be able to make good tackles, because this is your main job. If the ball carrier gets through the first line of defense—the linemen—you in the backfield are the last line of defense and must tackle the ball carrier before he can reach the goal line. If the play is a pass, you and the other backfield defenders must be able to intercept it or knock it to the ground.

The Backfield Stance

In playing in the backfield, you should not use the 3- or 4-point stance. If you did, you would not be able to see the offensive team well enough to read the play. You must stand up, but be ready to move fast. Use the backfield stance as described in Chapter 4. In this position, you can see everything taking place on the field, and are ready to start fast in any direction.

Reading the Offense

Defensive teams do not go onto the field without a plan. As you know from watching pro football, there are many different plans defensive teams use. One type might work well against one team, but not very well against another team. Coaches use movies and scouting reports to study other teams and the men on other teams for many hours before they decide what kind of a defense will work the best. It takes lots of practice and special skills to play each kind of defense, so it is enough to be able to play one kind well.

In our game, with only 4 or 5 men on each team, we can't use all the same defensive plans an 11-man team would use. But there is one general idea we can use. It is called "matching strength," which means that whatever the offensive team does, the defense must do something to stop them.

Should all the defensive men play on the line of scrimmage?

Should they all play on one side of the line of scrimmage?

How many should be in the backfield?

The answer to these questions, lies in being able to "read the offense" and match their strengths. First, you must be able to judge what they are going to do.

When watching a pro football game, remember how the defense "shifts" just before the ball is snapped? They are trying to get into the right place after seeing what the offensive team is going to do. Listen carefully the next time you watch a football game on TV and you might hear the defensive players yell to each other as the offensive team takes its place: "Strong Left!" or "Strong Right!" They are telling each other on which side of the line the offensive team is placing most of their men. Then they move around a little to match the strength on that side of the line. Or you might hear one of them yell: "Pass!" This means that they think the offensive team is getting ready to pass, so they move their backfield around to defend against it.

Sometimes the offensive team fools them. They make it look like they are going to pass, or call a certain line play, then they do something else before the

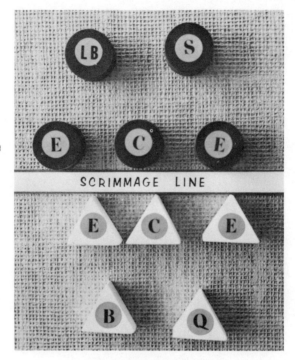

3-MAN DEFENSIVE LINE (dark figures) matching the T formation of the offense.

SCRIMMAGE LINE

defensive team can correct their mistake. So, it is important that defensive men learn how to read the offense, and match their strength.

The Three-Man Line

This is a good defensive plan if you have 5 men on a team. It gives strength to the scrimmage line to meet the strength of the offense and it leaves 2 in the backfield to protect against the long pass or the long run. One plays as a Linebacker and the other as a Safety.

If the offensive team looks like they are going to use a "T" formation, the two Ends play on the right and

Three-Man Line ◎ 127

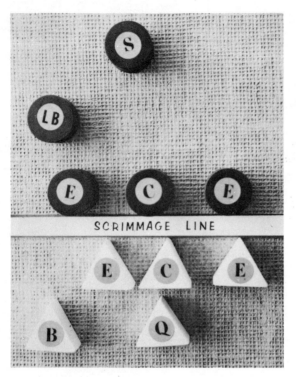

SCRIMMAGE LINE

3-MAN DEFENSIVE LINE with a strong left, matching the offense's single wing.

left side of the scrimmage line with the Center between them, and the Backs evenly placed.

If the offense is using a Single Wing formation, you can read the play as a "Strong Left" or a "Strong Right," and meet or match the strong side by putting both backfield players or even both Ends on that side.

The offensive team might be doing this to fool you, and will run the play to the weak side. If this happens, the Linebacker moves across rapidly to stop the runner before he can cross the line of scrimmage. The Safety helps by staying back in case the runner does get through or around the scrimmage line, or to defend against the pass if the run was a fake.

If you have only 4 men on a team, and you are certain that the offensive team is going to try to go through the scrimmage line, you can put 3 players on the line, just the same way as when you had a 5-man team, but you must remember that there will be only one player in the backfield. This will give you a very weak "last defense" line. The best this one backfield player can do is play as a Safety. He can't play as a Linebacker because the offensive team might throw a long pass over his head.

3-MAN LINE with a 4-man team on defense.

The Two-Man Line

This plan is not much use with a 5-man team, as it would make the line too weak. The offensive team could go through or around the scrimmage line too easily, but you can use it with a 4-man team. This would put 2 players on the scrimmage line and 2 in the backfield. In this case, the backfield should be placed so that one is closer to the scrimmage line to act as the Linebacker and the other one, a little farther back, is the Safety.

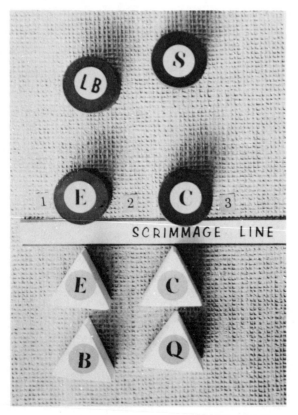

2-MAN LINE with a 4-man team on defense.

Goal Line Defense

When the offensive team gets close to the goal line, the scrimmage line must be strengthened. One way you can do this is to move a player from the backfield to the scrimmage line. You weaken the backfield, and you may need that player to defend against a pass. If you read the play as a running play, leave only one player in the backfield, and put the rest on the scrimmage line. If you read the play as a pass play, leave 2 men in the backfield and try to rush the passer.

Another way to strengthen the scrimmage line is to move the linemen closer together. You must be careful doing this as it makes the ends of the scrimmage line weak and a smart Quarterback will try to send the ball carrier around the end. When this happens, the Linebacker must move quickly to help stop the ball carrier at the line of scrimmage. Other placement of players will be needed in special situations.

Defending against a Pass

When the other team passes, there are three things you can do to stop it.

1. *Delay the receiver.* The End or a Back crashing through the line without the ball will usually be trying to get into position to become a pass receiver. If you can stop him or delay him from getting into that position, you have a good chance to stop the pass play. However, you must do this before the ball is in the air. Once the ball is in the air you must not touch him or it will be called "pass interference" and the pass will be called "complete" at the point you

touched the pass receiver. If you are playing on the line, don't let the End or a Running Back get through or by you. As the ball is snapped, charge into him using a shoulder charge, or any arm charge. Block him so he can't run. If you can keep him from going through the line, even for just a few seconds, he will not be able to get to where the Quarterback wants to throw the ball.

2. *Rush the passer.* If the Quarterback cannot throw the ball, the pass cannot be completed. Linemen should try to block the receiver going through the line, then rush the passer. If you only have 2 players on the line, one might rush the passer while the other tries to delay or stop the receiver. When rushing the passer, try to keep him from running with the ball, or getting away from the rush. Before the ball is snapped, talk it over with your teammates, and decide what you are going to do—who will rush the passer and who will delay the receiver. You have to play as a team.

3. *Intercepting a pass or knocking the ball down.* Once the pass is thrown, you have only one or two things left you can do—intercept or knock down the pass, or stop the receiver before he can go anywhere. You have to decide which to do. Don't let the receiver get behind you—keep him in front of you. If the pass is high, and you know you can either get it or knock it down, do it! Try it, especially if the pass is going over the goal line.

Another thing you must decide as a team is whether

to use a man-to-man defense against the pass, or whether to use a "zone defense." In a zone defense, each player has a certain area of the field he must defend, and must handle any passes or players that come into his area. If you have two players in the backfield, one must play a little closer to the scrimmage line than the other. He must defend the area behind the scrimmage line against short passes, such as a hook or a screen pass. The other man needs to play back a little further and be responsible for defending the area in front of the goal line against a long pass. The zone defense is usually best against a long pass, and where you have more than 2 or 3 players in the backfield.

If you only have 2 or 3 in the backfield, a man-to-man pass defense would probably be best. In this defense, each player on defense is assigned to watch a specific man on offense, and stay with him wherever he goes. If the offensive team has a player who is very fast, one of your men who is very fast ought to guard him. Each man on your defensive team has a man on the other team he must watch. The man-to-man defense is usually best to use against short passes and for teams with only 4 or 5 players.

Defending against the Punt or Kick

When the offensive team punts or kicks, the defensive team has two things to do: get the ball, and run it back toward the other goal line as far as they can. In order to do this, there should be two men in the defensive backfield. One player catches the ball and the other is his blocker as he runs downfield. It makes no difference how many men you have on your team—there should be 2 in the backfield on a punt or kick.

Running Back Punts and Kicks

When the other team punts or kicks, your team has a chance of getting some "easy" yards by moving the ball back up the field fast. The closer you can get the ball to the goal line, the easier it will be to score. The first thing you must do to have a good runback is to catch the ball. Get back far enough so you can run forward toward the falling ball, as it is almost impossible to catch a punted ball if you have to run backwards. Get under it and let it fall gently into your fingers, hands, and arms. Guide it with your hands and arms into your body, where you can hold it tightly. At times you might not want to run with the ball after you catch it. You can call for a "Fair Catch" by holding one arm and hand straight above your head before the ball gets to you. This means you can catch the ball without being bothered by players from the other team. But you must catch the ball. If you miss it or drop it, it is the same as a fumble and can be recovered by the other team.

On punts and kicks, always try to catch the ball. Don't let it bounce. Because of the shape of the ball, you are never sure which way it will bounce. You might not be able to get it, and it could bounce clear across your goal line. Or you might touch it without getting it and then it could be recovered by the other team as a fumble.

One man on your team should be given the job of catching the ball and running it back. He must play back far enough that the punter cannot kick the ball over his head. If it comes down before it gets to the goal line, he should try to catch it and run it back. If it comes down near or over the goal line, he should let it go. In our game, the ball would be brought out beyond the goal line 5 steps and placed in play.

As the ball is caught, the rest of your team should block for the runner. Before the ball is snapped, work out a plan. With 5 men on your team, you might have 2 run in front of the runner to block for him while the other 2 take their places near his side to block for him. If he runs straight down the sideline, you might place one or two runners in front of him and the others on his one side. The important things to remember about running back punts or kicks are: make a good catch, and then move as a team downfield.

Blocking Punts

When attempting to block punts, the linemen must try to charge through the line and get to the punter. They must aim their charge at the spot where the punter will be when he kicks the ball, not where he is standing when he gets it. Aim your charge at his kicking foot, and not his body. If you hit the punter's body while he is punting, he can be badly hurt. This is the reason there is such a stiff penalty for "Roughing the Kicker." So aim your charge at his foot and the ball and not his body.

TWO OTHER TYPES OF DEFENSE: Both formations use a 2-man line with a 5-man team, but the backfield is changed.

Team Charging

If you can read the offense as a running play, the entire line can charge together or "blitz," in the same direction to stop the play. For example, if you know the play is going to be a running play to the left, all the linemen can charge to the left. This will force the ball carrier out of bounds or stop him at the line of scrimmage. If you do read the play wrong, and all charge left while the runner goes right, he will get through or around the line easily. So you have to decide which way to do it. This you can do in your huddle or as the offensive team comes to the line of scrimmage. Try to decide which would be best—all charge left, charge right, charge in to the center, or charge straight—and do it as a team.

9. PLAYING WITH MORE THAN FIVE

Most of the time, you probably will be playing on a small field. If this is the case, you can have more fun with 3, 4, or 5 men on each team. If you have 12 boys who want to play, but have a small field, you might have three teams with 4 boys on each team and work out a plan whereby one team plays the winner of a game between the other two. You might also have four teams of 3 each and start two games with the winners of the two games playing for the "championship."

There may be times when you have a large field and can play with more boys on each team. The more boys you have on a team the more formations you can use. Placing 3 in the backfield and the rest on the scrimmage line probably works best most of the time. With 3 in the backfield, you can use almost any of the formations. You can line up across the field in a "T" formation with the snap going to any of the 3 and the other 2 working as blockers. You can use a "Single Wing" with the Quarterback working right behind the Center. You could use an "I" formation or put the Quarterback right behind the Center with the other 2 on either side and use a "Wishbone" formation. With any of these formations you can use different pass plays, option plays, lateral plays, screen plays, and hand-off plays.

10. EQUIPMENT

It is dangerous to play football without wearing special clothing and equipment. Good equipment is expensive. Some bad equipment is expensive also, and you should know how to tell good from bad.

The Football

This is discussed fully in Chapter One. Read it.

An Athletic Supporter

When boys reach the age of 9 or 10, the parts of their bodies between their legs should be protected from getting hurt in games such as football. Getting hit there can be very painful and can cause damage. To help prevent this, you should wear an athletic supporter. It should be purchased in a size that fits you—it doesn't cost very much. A "cup," made of plastic or stiff fiberboard which fits inside the athletic supporter, is needed by older boys.

Shoes

Basketball shoes with a good arch support that covers the ankles are good. Don't get shoes with

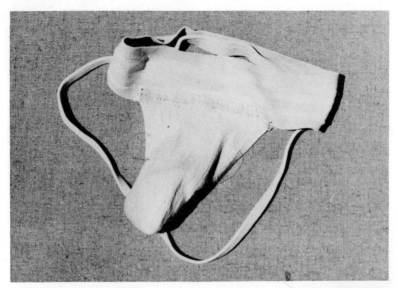

ATHLETIC SUPPORTER: All boys should wear a strap like this when playing football.

cleats, or those with long, hard plastic or metal "corks" for this game. There is too much danger of hurting someone. Sneakers with good soles and arch supports would be all right, but if possible get the kind which cover the ankle.

Helmet

In playing tackle football, the helmet is a necessary piece of equipment. Years ago, they were made of leather and weren't very well padded. Today they are made of tough plastic and are padded. First of all, look at the pads around the bottom of the helmet. They should be of a soft spongy material with a wax-

HELMETS are made of heavy plastic. Be sure yours has a good chin strap to hold it tightly on your head, yet make it easily removable. All helmets today have a 2-bar face guards and should have wax-smooth pads on the inside with a heavy suspended pad fastened in the top.

smooth, tough surface—a smooth surface which keeps the spongy material from soaking up sweat and water. Don't get any other kind.

The helmet should have a padded earhole so you can hear.

The pads in the top of the helmet should be made of the same material as the pads around the bottom and glued to the helmet. They might also be sewn to heavy elastic belting which is riveted to the helmet in what is called a "suspension" padding. If you get

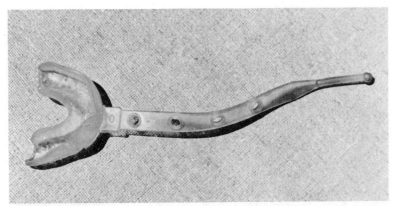

MOUTH GUARD: Made of soft plastic, this guard prevents your teeth and tongue from being injured. The type to get is the one with the tail which fastens to your chin strap and can't be lost.

this type, make sure the webbing is heavy and attached to the helmet so that no sharp rivets are showing.

The helmet should also have attached to it a good, plastic-covered face guard with two bars. This face guard should not be removable, but should be part of the helmet.

The helmet should also have a good chin strap with a large, strong snap-fastener which will hold the helmet on tightly, but which can also be unfastened easily.

Mouth Guard

This is usually made of soft, clear plastic, and fits inside the mouth over the teeth. It can be fitted and purchased from a dentist, or can be purchased from

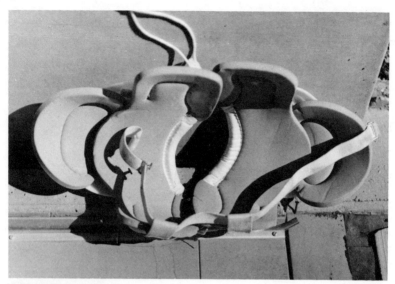

SHOULDER PADS (bottom view): Here you can see the lower and upper padding, as well as the cloth belt that goes around your chest. It hooks to the front of the pads to hold them in place close to your body.

a sporting goods store. The plastic material is soft enough so that you can bite down hard the first time you wear it to "fit" it to your teeth. It will then hold that shape. Get the kind with a "tail" which you can fasten to your chin strap, so you can take it out without dropping or losing it.

Shoulder Pads and Jersey

If you are going to play tackle football, you must have a set of shoulder pads and a jersey to cover them.

SHOULDER PADS (top view): Note the smooth padding and bending around the neck hole. The pads should cover the upper part of your chest too, and your upper arms. The plastic leaf gives extra protection to the upper and lower pads.

The shoulder pads will help protect you and the jersey, or shirt, will hold the shoulder pads in place and keep them from moving around and getting damaged. Don't wear shoulder pads without the jersey, which should be knit, with a long shirttail and made especially for this.

The most important thing about shoulder pads, is to make sure they fit you comfortably. Try them on, and have someone who knows how to do it, check them for size. They should be made with a strong plastic top, with a soft, spongy pad underneath. Each shoulder should be covered with two pads hinged together. One pad goes on the bottom and fits closely around your neck, with a smooth neckline, and covers the top part of your chest and back. The top pad is hinged to the bottom pad, and is long enough to cover the shoulder and just a small part of the upper arms. A good shoulder pad will also have another plastic leaf over both of these pads to cover the hinge. The right and left pads, should be held together with laces front and back, and the back set of laces should be laced and tied. The front set of laces could be laced and tied like the back, but it would be better if you have some way to lace them up and loosen them quickly yourself.

To hold the whole set of shoulder pads tightly against the body, usually a cloth belt fits around the upper part of your chest, and this can be easily tightened or released. This belt runs through loops attached to the pads themselves with some sort of a buckle or fastener on the front. Wear a pull-over, or T-shirt under the shoulder pads to keep them from making your skin sore.

Hip Pads

There are two kinds of hip pads. One kind straps to your body, and has two pads, one to fit over each hip, with one between them which fits in back over your tail bone . . . all tied together with a belt. You strap these on then pull your pants on over them.

The other kind, which is attached to your pants, is

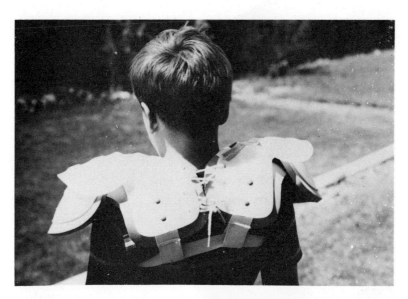

SHOULDER PADS: These lace in front and back, and have a belt that holds them down.

the kind most boys wear. They don't cost as much, are easier to put on, and easier to take care of. There is a pad for each hip and one for the tail bone. The pads of each type should be made of soft spongy material which won't soak up sweat and water. The ones attached to the pants have big snap fasteners so they can be taken off while the pants are being washed. Of course these must be purchased with the pants.

It is important to wear hip pads above the hip bone to prevent injuries to the top of the hip bone called "pointers."

Pants

Football pants come in two types also—one with pads and one without pads. As explained above, most boys wear the kind *with* the hip pads. But, either kind must have pads over the upper part of your leg, and under your knee, and fit tightly to hold the pads in the right place.

The pad that fits over the upper and front part of your leg should be made of hard plastic, be curved to fit your leg and covered with a soft spongy material. These fit inside your pants leg in a special pocket and can be easily removed so the pants can be washed. Football pants should be long enough to cover your knee, with a pad which fits just below the knee. This pad should be soft and also removable when the pants are washed.

The pants are usually made of nylon and cotton,

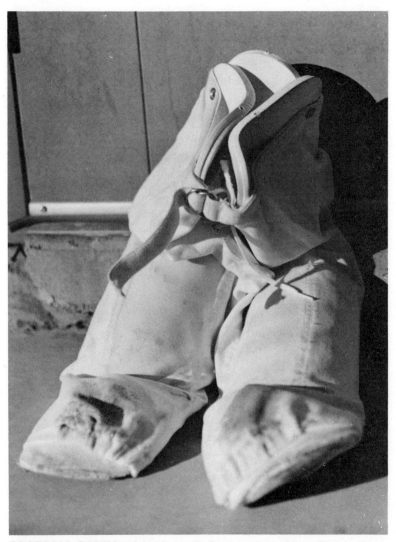

FOOTBALL PANTS with hip pads fastened to them. The pads go over your tailbone. Inside the pants are hard, moulded pads covered with a soft, spongy material to cover your thighs, as well as soft pads that fit under your knees. Notice the ring-type buckle.

are washable and strong. The belt, of cloth, should be part of the pants with a rounded buckle or two smooth, round rings which are better than a buckle. Large buckles are dangerous and a separate belt is easy to lose. The pants should have laces in front, rather than buttons or zippers, so they can be laced tight, and yet stretch for a good fit, so they will hold all the pads in place and not fall down.

GLOSSARY

(See page 82 for special rules)

BACKFIELD IN MOTION: Any movement of the backs after the team has taken its position and before the snap of the ball. In regular football, one of the eleven men may move before the ball is snapped, but he must not move forward.

BLOCKING: Using your body legally to keep a defensive man from making a tackle or to move him away from the ball or action.

BOMB: A long pass intended for a touchdown.

CHARGE, CRASH: The act of moving hard and fast into the line of scrimmage as the ball is snapped.

CORNERBACK: A man who plays in the backfield on defense just behind the linebackers.

CLIPPING: Blocking a man other than the ball carrier from behind. Since he has no way to defend himself, and could be hurt when someone hits him from behind, clipping is against the rules.

DOWN: A play or a try by the offensive team to move the football toward the goal line. In regular football rules, a team has four downs in which to gain 10 yards (to make a touchdown).

END: The player on the end of the scrimmage line.

If he plays close to the next player on the line, he is a "tight" End. If he plays some distance away from the next player on the scrimmage line, he is a "split" End.

FAKE: To move in such a way as to make another man, or team, think you are going to do one thing, then do another.

FORWARD PASS: A pass thrown toward the goal line. It cannot be thrown from in front of the line of scrimmage.

FUMBLE: A dropped ball that anyone can get and "recover."

HAND-OFF: Passing or exchanging the ball from one player to another at very close range.

"I" FORMATION: A team on offense has its back-field men all lined up behind each other in a straight line.

INTERCEPTION: Catching a pass thrown by the other team.

KICK-OFF: Placing the ball on the ground on a tee or having a teammate hold it while it is kicked at the beginning of each quarter of a football game or after a team scores.

LATERAL PASS: A pass thrown or tossed sideways or slightly backwards across the field. If thrown from in front of the line of scrimmage, a pass may not move forward through the air toward the goal line.

LINEBACKER: This defensive man plays in the back-field, but close enough to the line of scrimmage that he can help the linemen to keep the ball carrier from getting through or around the scrimmage line.

LINEMAN: Any man who plays on the line of scrimmage in the position of Center, Guards, Tackles, or Ends.

MATCHING STRENGTH: Placing defensive men on the line where they can face or meet the offensive team equally. For example, if the offensive team has three players on one side of the scrimmage line, the defensive team places the same number on that side also.

OFFSIDE: When players jump over the scrimmage line before the ball is snapped, they are offside. The penalty in regular football is 5 yards.

PLACE KICK: In an attempt to score by kicking a field goal (through goal posts) one player usually catches the snap from the Center and holds the ball with one end of it on the ground while the kicker kicks it. In regular football, this can be done at any point of the ball game and is worth 3 points. When kicked the same way following a touchdown, it is worth only one point.

PUNT: This is a kick in which the ball is held by the player who kicks it without help.

QUARTERBACK: The player in the offensive backfield who calls the signals and decides which play to try. Usually he is the one to take the ball from the Center when it is snapped.

READING THE OFFENSE: Deciding what the team

on the offense is going to do. You might "read" it as a pass play or as a running play.

RECEIVER: The player who catches or tries to catch a pass.

RUNNING BACK: One of the players in the offensive backfield, who runs or receives passes, as distinguished from the Quarterback.

SAFETYMAN: The furthest-back player in the backfield on defense to defend the goal line against long passes and ball carriers who get through the scrimmage line and through the backfield.

SCREEN PASS: A pass play in which the defensive linemen are faked into thinking the passer will be thrown for a loss, but the passer tosses the ball over their heads to a waiting receiver.

SCRIMMAGE LINE: An invisible line running across the football field and through one end of the football as it is placed on the ground ready for play. There are actually two scrimmage lines—one for each team—one through each end of the football. The space between these two invisible lines is called the "neutral zone." No part of the body, hands, or feet may be in this neutral zone until after the ball is snapped.

SHIFT: The act of moving from one position to another before the ball is snapped. A lineman cannot shift after taking a position. No part of his body can move. The defensive backfield players may shift at any time, but they must do it and remain motionless for at least one second before the ball is snapped.

SINGLE WING: A formation used by some teams on offense. It has many forms, but is identified by the way an End or a Back takes his position to the side of the formation. When he is off by himself, he is called a "Wing-back" and the formation is called a "Single Wing."

SNAP: The act of moving the ball from the neutral zone and starting the play. The Center does this, usually on a signal from the Quarterback and he usually gives it to the Quarterback, except on punts.

STANCE: A special way a player gets ready to move as the ball is snapped. (See page 54.)

STRAIGHT ARM or STIFF ARM: This is a means used by a ball carrier to defend himself against a tackler. He may use his open hand and arm to push a tackler out of the way and away from him. He cannot use his fist to strike the tackler.

TACKLING: Dragging a ball carrier to the ground.

TEE: A small device placed on the ground to hold the ball while it is being kicked.

"T" FORMATION: This is a formation used by an offensive team in which all the backs are lined up to the side of each other in a straight line and parallel to the line of scrimmage. A line drawn through them, crossing one drawn from the Center to the Quarterback, forms the letter "T."

TOUCHDOWN: The act of moving the football over the defensive team's goal line on the ground or through the air. This is the main objective of all football games.

TRAP: This occurs when a charging lineman is faked

into thinking he is getting through the scrimmage line easily. Then at the "right" moment, he is blocked where he cannot move to stop a play.

YARDAGE: Football fields are usually measured in yards. The distance an offensive team moves the ball down the field toward the goal line is measured in yards.

INDEX

arm, straight or stiff 153
athletic supporter 140, 141

"B" plays 106–109
backfield 125
   defensive 124–125
   offensive 90–91
   stance 61–62
"backfield in motion" 54, 151
"basket" for the hand-off 25–27
behind tackle 71
"blitz," defensive 137
blocking 72–79, 114–115, 119, 151
   body 75–77
   offensive 89
   practice 79–81
   shoulder 72, 74, 75
body block 75–77
"bomb" pass 112–113, 151

catching passes, general rules 35
catching the long pass 30, 31–34
Center
   full pass 34–35
   "snap" 19–24, 153
   stance 21, 60–61
charge, arm 122

charging the line 120–122, 137, 151
cleats 141
clipping 151
Cornerback 151
crashing the line 36–38, 120, 151

defensive play 117–137
   backfield 124–125
   formations 127–130
   goal-line 131
   linemen 120–123
   pass 131–133
   punt 133–135
   rules 118–120
downs 151
   number of 84

end run 104, 105, 108
Ends 151–152
   defensive 123–124
equipment 64, 140–150
exercises, strengthening 14, 18, 78–81

"fair catch" 134
fake 152